DAY HIKES ON
OAHU

57 GREAT HIKES

by Robert Stone

Day Hike Books, Inc.

RED LODGE, MONTANA

Published by Day Hike Books, Inc.
P.O. Box 865
Red Lodge, Montana 59068

Distributed by The Globe Pequot Press
246 Goose Lane
P.O. Box 480
Guilford, CT 06437-0480
800-243-0495 (direct order) · 800-820-2329 (fax order)
www.globe-pequot.com

Photographs by Robert Stone
Design by Paula Doherty

The author has made every attempt to provide accurate information in this book. However, trail routes and features may change—please use common sense and forethought, and be mindful of your own capabilities. Let this book guide you, but be aware that each hiker assumes responsibility for their own safety. The author and publisher do not assume any responsibility for loss, damage or injury caused through the use of this book.

Cover photo: Sacred Falls, Hike 53
Back cover photo: Lighthouse on Makapuu Point, Hike 1

Table of Contents

THE HIKES

Southeast Coast and Waikiki

Mount Tantalus Trails
(Honolulu Mauka Trail System)

Honolulu to Kailua
Kailua Bay and Waimanalo Bay

Central Oahu

West Coast and Waimea Bay

The Windward Coast

About the Hikes

Many of Oahu's most beautiful and unique attractions are easily accessible by foot. A hike along the coast or into the backcountry will most certainly enhance your time spent on this tropical island. *Day Hikes on Oahu* takes you to 57 of this island's best hikes. The entire coastline is included as well as scenic high-country hikes in the Koolau Mountains. All levels of hiking experience are accommodated, from easy beach strolls to mountain climbs that reward the hiker with sweeping views. Each hike includes a map, detailed driving and hiking directions and a summary. An overall map of Oahu and the locations of the hikes is found on the next page.

The Hawaiian Islands are among the most beautiful and dramatic tropical landscapes on earth. The islands are 500 miles from any other island and 2,500 miles from the nearest continent. The landscape is covered with verdant green mountains, active and dormant craters, remote canyons, lush flora and fauna, countless waterfalls, colored sand beaches and coral reefs. Warm, turquoise ocean water surrounds the islands. The temperature hovers around 80 degrees with sunshine and gentle winds. Trade winds buffet the northeast side of each island, creating dense rain forests and exotic tropical plants. The southwest region of each island has barren desert-like terrain covered with cactus plants. Oahu offers easy access to swimming, snorkeling, diving, windsurfing, boating, fishing, bicycling, sunbathing, people watching and, of course, hiking.

These hikes offer a variety of lush valleys, spectacular waterfalls, volcanic craters, gardens, tropical swimming holes, coastal beaches, tidepools, ridge trails and intimate rainforest hikes. To help you decide which hikes are most appealing to you, a brief summary of the highlights is included with each hike. You may enjoy these areas for a short time or the whole day.

Oahu houses more than 70 percent of the Hawaiian Islands' population and is also the most popular tourist destination. When most people think of Oahu, they imagine the capital city of Honolulu with its world-famous skyline and the white sand beaches of Waikiki. Diamond Head, a 760-foot crater at the west end of Waikiki, has sweeping views of the city from its summit. (Hike 6 leads into the crater and up to its summit.)

Oahu has much more to offer, however, than Honolulu and the beaches of Waikiki. The many hiking trails which take you away from the crowds showcase the island's natural beauty. The Koolau Mountains, for example, only two miles north of Waikiki, contain a network of hiking trails in the rain forest and along mountain ridges and valleys. The views from atop the Pali Lookout (Hike 23) are incredible.

The east coast of Oahu has a variety of beautiful sandy beaches and jagged, steep mountains. The charming, small communities of Kailua and Kaneohe can be visited on the way to the coastal hikes along the windward coast. Kahana Valley, inland from the town of Kahana, is a 5,000-acre forest with picnic areas, hiking trails and cultural shrines (Hikes 54—56).

Take time to visit the north shore and leeward coast, where there is one beautiful beach after another. This area is known for its great surfing and the world-class waves of the Banzai Pipeline, Sunset Beach and Waimea Bay. The Waianae Mountains and 4,000-foot Mount Kaala dominate the landscape behind these beaches. Coastal hikes along the leeward coast include undisturbed tidepools, sandy coves and jungle valleys. Puu O Mahuka Heiau, Oahu's oldest temple and once used for human sacrifice, has beautiful, panoramic views (Hike 46). Hikes 41 and 42 on Kaena Point, the westernmost peninsula of Oahu, includes tidepools, sea caves, arches, blowholes, dunes and a crashing surf along the volcanic coastline.

A few basic necessities will make your hike more enjoyable. Bring hats, sunscreen, insect repellent, sunglasses, snacks and drinking water. The trails can be (and usually are) slippery due to rain and mud. Use caution and wear shoes with a grip. Bring swimsuits and outdoor gear to use at the coast.

Enjoy your hike and the beautiful scenery that unfolds along the trails!

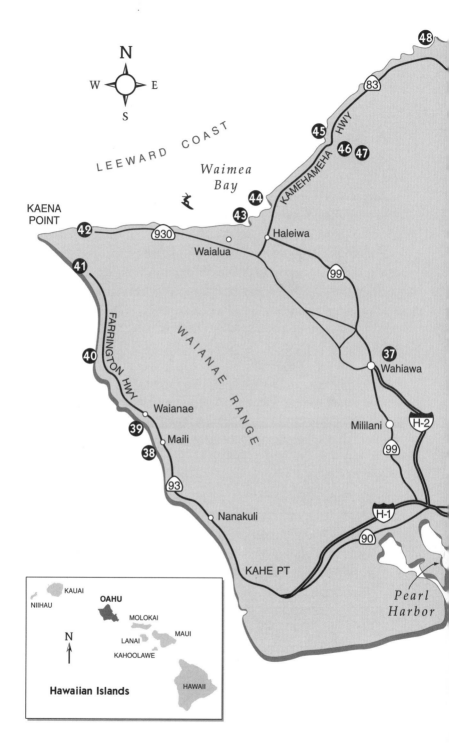

N

W E

S

LEEWARD COAST

48

83

KAMEHAMEHA HWY

45

46 47

Waimea
Bay

44

KAENA
POINT

42

43

930

Waialua

Haleiwa

99

41

FARRINGTON HWY

40

37

Wahiawa

WAIANAE RANGE

Waianae

Mililani

H-2

39

Maili

38

99

93

H-1

Nanakuli

90

KAHE PT

Pearl
Harbor

KAUAI

NIIHAU

OAHU

MOLOKAI

N

LANAI

MAUI

KAHOOLAWE

Hawaiian Islands

HAWAII

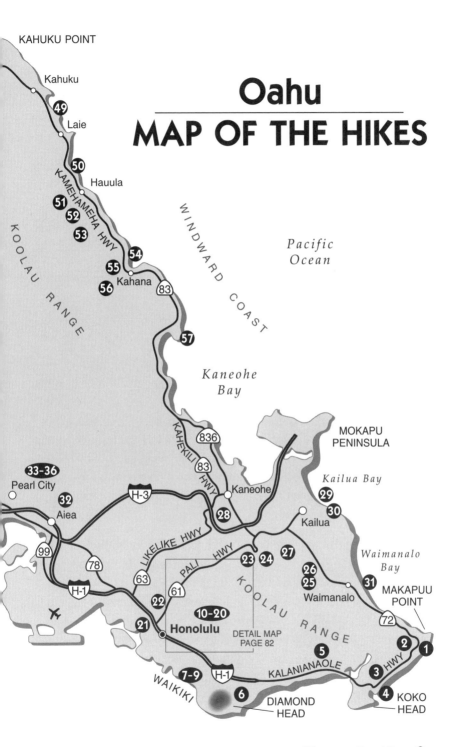

KAHUKU POINT

Kahuku

49

Laie

50

Hauula

51

52

53

KAMEHAMEHA HWY

54

55
Kahana

56

83

KOOLAU RANGE

WINDWARD COAST

Pacific Ocean

Oahu
MAP OF THE HIKES

57

Kaneohe Bay

KAHEKILI HWY

836

83

Kaneohe

MOKAPU PENINSULA

Kailua Bay

29

30

Kailua

33-36
Pearl City

32
Aiea

H-3

28

LIKELIKE HWY

PALI HWY

23 **24** **27**

26
25
Waimanalo

Waimanalo Bay

31

MAKAPUU POINT

99

78

63

61

22

H-1

21

10-20
Honolulu

DETAIL MAP
PAGE 82

KOOLAU RANGE

72

7-9 **H-1**

6

WAIKIKI

KALANIANAOLE

5

2 **1**

3 HWY

4 KOKO HEAD

DIAMOND HEAD

Hike 1
Makapuu State Wayside

Hiking distance: 2 miles round trip
Hiking time: 1.25 hour
Elevation gain: 550 feet
Maps: U.S.G.S. Koko Head
Oahu Reference Maps: Honolulu/Oahu South Shore

Summary of hike: Makapuu State Wayside sits on the easternmost tip of Oahu. This trail, a former lighthouse access road, leads to majestic vistas on Makapuu Point. From the 600-foot ocean bluff are two observation decks, World War II bunkers and a working lighthouse (photo on back cover). Off the shore from the steep cliffs are Manana "Rabbit" Island, an old volcanic crater, and Kaohikaipu "Turtle" Island, both state seabird sanctuaries. Makapuu Point is also an excellent whale watching site.

Driving directions: From McCully Street and King Street in Waikiki, go east on King Street one mile. Curve left and enter H-1 east. Continue 12.8 miles to the trailhead pullout. It is located 4.1 miles beyond the Hanauma Bay turnoff. (Along the way, H-1 becomes the Lunalilo Freeway, which becomes the Kalanianaole Highway/72.) As the highway gains elevation toward the saddle between Makapuu Head and the rest of Oahu, you will see a narrow, paved walking trail head off to the right. Park alongside the road.

Hiking directions: Walk up the paved and gated road, steadily heading uphill towards Makapuu Head. The trail passes through two gates and lichen-covered boulders along the way. Koko Crater and Koko Head are prominent in the southwest. As the trail joins the cliff's edge at Puu o Kipahulu, curve left and head north, parallel to the eroded cliffs overlooking the coastline. As the trail levels out, curve left toward the bunkers at the summit. To the right are the two observation platforms. The lighthouse is 100 feet below near Makapuu Point. After marveling at the panoramic vistas, return along the same route

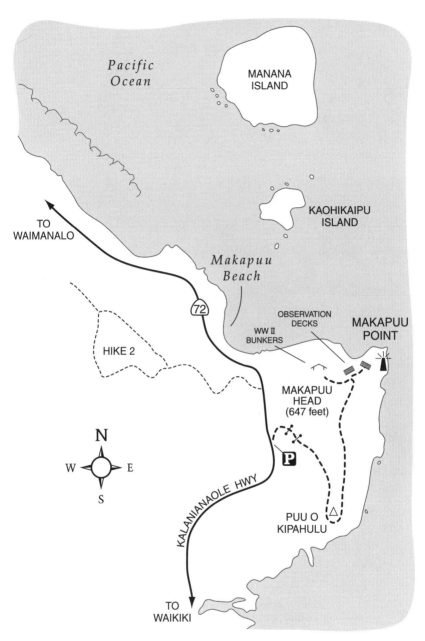

Pacific Ocean

MANANA ISLAND

KAOHIKAIPU ISLAND

TO WAIMANALO

Makapuu Beach

72

OBSERVATION DECKS

WW II BUNKERS

MAKAPUU POINT

HIKE 2

MAKAPUU HEAD (647 feet)

N

W E

S

P

PUU O KIPAHULU

KALANIANAOLE HWY

TO WAIKIKI

MAKAPUU
STATE WAYSIDE

Hike 2
Makapuu Hang Glider Trail

Hiking distance: 1.5 mile loop
Hiking time: 1 hour
Elevation gain: 600 feet
Maps: U.S.G.S. Koko Head
Oahu Reference Maps: Honolulu/Oahu South Shore

Summary of hike: The Makapuu Hang Glider Trail is an unmaintained trail across the highway from Makapuu Head (Hike 1). The trail is used by hang gliders to reach several launching sites. The extensive coastal views sweep across the cliffs from Kaneohe Bay to Koko Head.

Driving directions: From McCully Street and King Street in Waikiki, go east on King Street one mile. Curve left and enter H-1 east. Continue 12.9 miles to the trailhead pullout. It is located 4.2 miles beyond the Hanauma Bay turnoff. (Along the way, H-1 becomes the Lunalilo Freeway, which becomes the Kalanianaole Highway/72.) As the highway gains elevation between Makapuu Head and the rest of Oahu, you will see a trail on the left, just before reaching the left bend in the road at the top of the hill. Park alongside the road.

Hiking directions: The unsigned trail is to the right of the fenced area. Head up the rocky path, gaining elevation to a trail split at 0.3 miles. Bear left to a ridge with fantastic views of Koko Crater and the ocean at a half mile. Follow the ridge loop to the right, reaching one of the hang gliding jump sites. The panoramic views extend from Kaneohe Bay to the islands of Manana and Kaohikaipu. To return, follow the ridge northeast towards Manana Island. Curve to the east and steeply descend, completing the loop. Retrace your steps to the left.

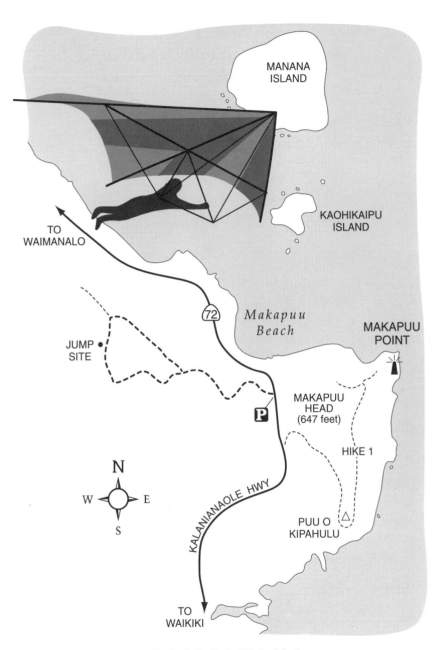

MANANA
ISLAND

KAOHIKAIPU
ISLAND

TO
WAIMANALO

72

*Makapuu
Beach*

MAKAPUU
POINT

JUMP
SITE

P

MAKAPUU
HEAD
(647 feet)

HIKE 1

N

W   E

S

KALANIANAOLE HWY

PUU O
KIPAHULU

TO
WAIKIKI

MAKAPUU
HANG GLIDER TRAIL

Hike 3
Koko Crater Botanic Garden
408 Kealahou Street
Open daily from sunrise to sunset

Hiking distance: 2.5 mile loop
Hiking time: 1.5 hours
Elevation gain: 100 feet
Maps: U.S.G.S. Koko Head
Oahu Reference Maps: Honolulu/Oahu South Shore
Koko Crater Botanical Garden map

Summary of hike: Koko Crater, historically known as Kohelepelepe, is a dormant, steep-walled cinder cone near the east end of Oahu. Inside the 200-acre crater is a 60-acre botanic garden, still in the early stages of development. The trail loops through the garden around the perimeter of the crater basin. The garden cultivates rare dryland plants, endangered native flora and includes plants from the Americas, Africa and Madagascar. The blooming groves of plumeria and bougainvillea are diverse and rich with color and fragrance.

Driving directions: From McCully Street and King Street in Waikiki, go east on King Street one mile. Curve left and enter H-1 east. Continue 11.2 miles to Kealahou Street. It is located 2.5 miles beyond the Hanauma Bay turnoff. (Along the way, H-1 becomes the Lunalilo Freeway, which becomes the Kalanianaole Highway/72.) Turn left on Kealahou Street, and drive 0.6 miles to the signed turnoff. Turn left and continue 0.4 miles to the botanic garden at the end of the road.

Hiking directions: Walk through the entrance gate, and take the path to the right between the plumeria and bougainvillea groves. At a quarter mile is a trail split, beginning the loop. Follow the right fork past a multicolored hibiscus grove and the cacti. At the west end of the crater, in the Hawaiian plant section, is a signed junction. The left fork heads downhill on the Inner Loop. The right fork heads uphill on the Outer Loop. Both of the trails merge further ahead. After the trails rejoin, complete the loop, returning to the trailhead adjacent to the Koko Crater stables.

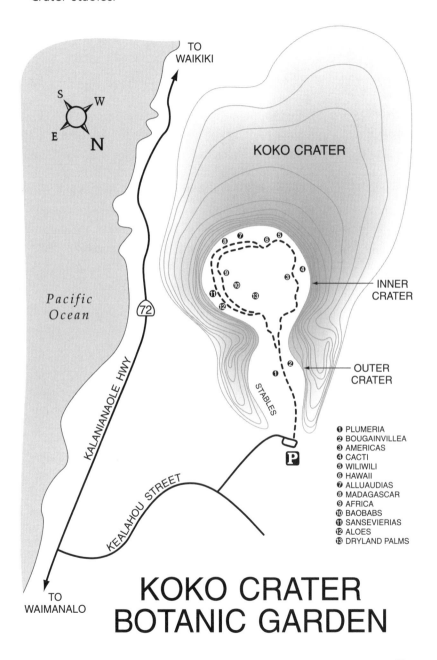

TO
WAIKIKI

KOKO CRATER

INNER
CRATER

OUTER
CRATER

Pacific
Ocean

72

KALANIANAOLE HWY

STABLES

P

KEALAHOU STREET

TO
WAIMANALO

❶ PLUMERIA
❷ BOUGAINVILLEA
❸ AMERICAS
❹ CACTI
❺ WILIWILI
❻ HAWAII
❼ ALLUAUDIAS
❽ MADAGASCAR
❾ AFRICA
❿ BAOBABS
⓫ SANSEVIERIAS
⓬ ALOES
⓭ DRYLAND PALMS

KOKO CRATER
BOTANIC GARDEN

Hike 4
Hanauma Bay to the Toilet Bowl

Hiking distance: 1.4 miles round trip
Hiking time: 1 hour
Elevation gain: 100 feet
Maps: U.S.G.S. Koko Head
       Oahu Reference Maps: Central Oahu/Windward Coast

Summary of hike: Hanauma Bay is surrounded by volcanic cliffs, palm trees and a half mile of white sand. The calm, shallow water in the bay make it a popular snorkeling area, abundant with coral reefs and fish. Along the east edge of the bay is a raised terrace. The trail runs along this ledge, passing tidepools and splashing waves to the Toilet Bowl. This natural, 30-foot round hole along the rock terrace fills and empties as the waves wash in and out, resembling a flushing toilet. Hanauma Bay was a filming location for Elvis Presley in *Blue Hawaii* and Burt Lancaster in *From Here To Eternity*.

Driving directions: From McCully Street and King Street in Waikiki, go east on King Street one mile. Curve left and enter H-1 east. Continue 8.7 miles to the Hanauma Bay turnoff on the right. (Along the way, H-1 becomes Lunalilo Freeway which becomes Kalanianaole Highway/72.) Turn right and drive 0.3 miles into the parking lot. A parking fee and entrance fee are required.

Hiking directions: From the parking lot, pass the entrance station. Descend along a paved walkway to the bay. At the beach, go to the east side (left) of the bay to the raised rock ledge. Follow the rock terrace towards Palea Point. Walk around the first point to the alcove. At the back of this inlet is the Toilet Bowl. Any further, the ocean waves and current become dangerous along the ledge. Return along the same path.

    CAUTION: Unexpected waves splash onto the path. During high tide, it is not advisable to hike here as the waves can sweep you away. Caution signs are posted.

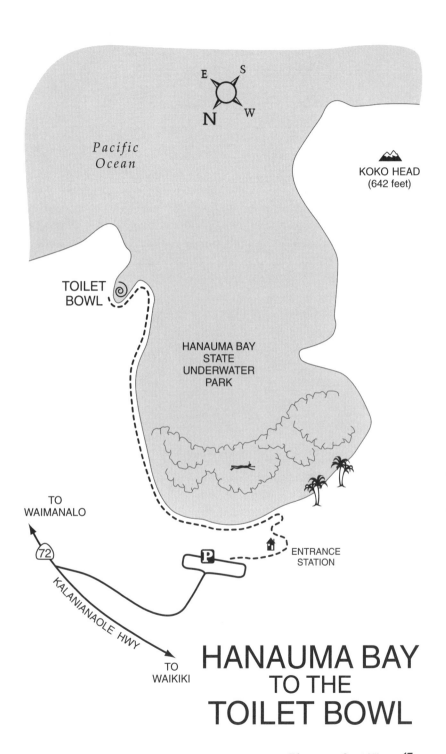

Pacific
Ocean

KOKO HEAD
(642 feet)

TOILET
BOWL

HANAUMA BAY
STATE
UNDERWATER
PARK

TO
WAIMANALO

72

KALANIANAOLE HWY

P

ENTRANCE
STATION

TO
WAIKIKI

HANAUMA BAY
TO THE
TOILET BOWL

Hike 5
Kuliouou Valley Trail

Hiking distance: 1.4 miles round trip
Hiking time: 45 minutes
Elevation gain: 300 feet
Maps: U.S.G.S. Koko Head
       Oahu Reference Maps: Honolulu/Oahu South Shore

Summary of hike: The Kuliouou Valley Trail is an easy, pastoral hike located a short distance east of Waikiki. The shaded trail parallels Kuliouou Stream up the right side of this lush valley. The path leads to the head of the narrow valley through an exotic forest with an abundance of moss-covered rocks.

Driving directions: From McCully Street and King Street in Waikiki, go east on King Street one mile. Curve left and enter H-1 east. Continue 6.5 miles to Kuliouou Road. (Along the way, H-1 becomes the Lunalilo Freeway, which becomes the Kalanianaole Highway/72.) Turn left on Kuliouou Road and drive one mile to Kalaau Place. Turn right and park in the cul-de-sac 0.2 miles ahead.

Hiking directions: The posted trailhead is located at the end of the cul-de sac. Begin by walking down the paved road about 50 yards. The footpath heads off to the right past a hunter check-in station and down to Kuliouou Stream. At 0.3 miles is a junction with the Kuliouou Ridge Trail on the right. The Ridge Trail switchbacks 900 feet out of the valley to the ridge above (1.2 miles to the picnic shelter). Continue straight ahead on the Kuliouou Valley Trail, following the contours of the hillside above the stream. At 0.8 miles, the trail meets the streambed. This is the turnaround spot. However, you can continue a short distance further to the valley's end up a less defined path. Return along the same trail.

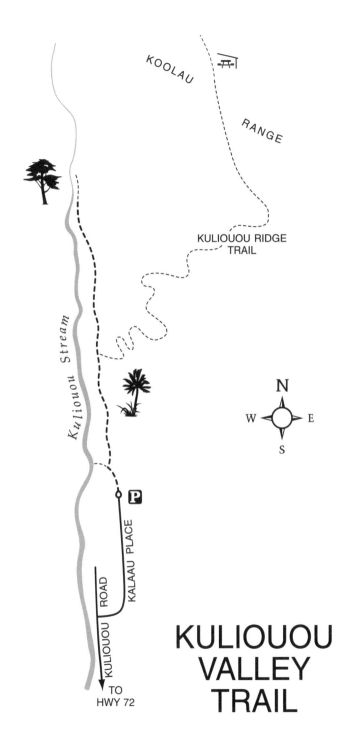

KOOLAU

RANGE

KULIOUOU RIDGE
TRAIL

Kuliouou Stream

N
W   E
S

P

KALAAU PLACE

KULIOUOU ROAD

TO
HWY 72

KULIOUOU
VALLEY
TRAIL

Hike 6
Diamond Head

Hiking distance: 1.5 miles round trip
Hiking time: 1 hour
Elevation gain: 550 feet
Maps: U.S.G.S. Honolulu
   Oahu Reference Maps: Honolulu/Oahu South Shore

Summary of hike: Diamond Head, known to Hawaiians as Leahi, is recognized as Hawaii's most famous landmark. Once used as a military observation station, the dormant volcano is now a state monument. The trail crosses the crater floor and climbs past several scenic overlooks, reaching the 762-foot summit at Point Leahi with postcard-perfect views. From the bunker atop the summit are incredible 365-degree panoramic vistas of Waikiki, Honolulu, Punchbowl, Koko Head, Koko Crater, the Leeward Coast and the blue Pacific.

Driving directions: From Waikiki, head southeast on Kalakaua Avenue, the main street running through Waikiki. Near the east end, at Kapiolani Park, curve to the left at a road split onto Monsarrat Avenue. Monsarrat Avenue becomes Diamond Head Road. Drive along the north side of the massive crater to the signed Diamond Head State Monument. Turn right. Follow the entrance road through a tunnel to the trailhead parking lot.

Hiking directions: Take the paved walkway to the signed trailhead by the restrooms. Head gently uphill along the interior crater floor towards the cliffs at the southwest rim of the cone. The path ascends the crater wall to an overlook of the crater's interior. Climb steps to the entrance of a dark 225-foot tunnel. Walk through the tunnel using the railing as a guide. Once through the tunnel, begin climbing the 99 cement steps, reaching an observation room and a spiral staircase. Wind up the staircase to the World War II bunker at the top. Climb out of the dark bunker to the stunning views of Oahu. To the left are observation platforms at Point Leahi. Return along the same trail.

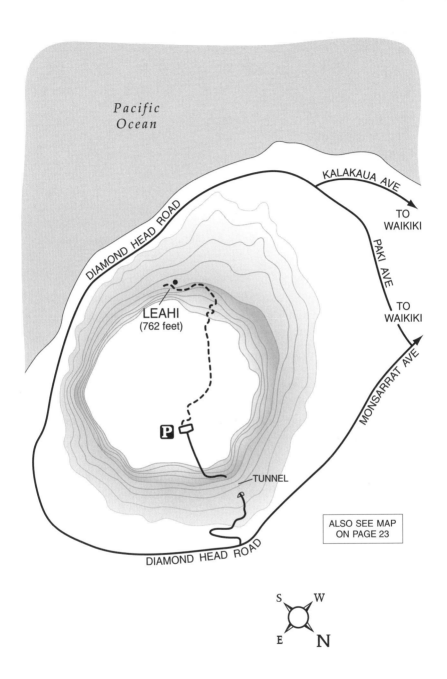

Pacific
Ocean

KALAKAUA AVE

TO
WAIKIKI

DIAMOND HEAD ROAD

PAKI AVE

LEAHI
(762 feet)

TO
WAIKIKI

MONSARRAT AVE

P

TUNNEL

ALSO SEE MAP
ON PAGE 23

DIAMOND HEAD ROAD

DIAMOND HEAD

Hike 7
Waikiki Beach to Kapiolani Park

Hiking distance: 4 miles round trip
Hiking time: 2 hours
Elevation gain: Level
Maps: U.S.G.S. Honolulu
      Oahu Reference Maps: Honolulu/Oahu South Shore

Summary of hike: Waikiki Beach is a series of smaller white sand beaches extending along this fabled oceanfront shoreline, with picnic areas, concession stands, water sport rentals, luxury hotels, shady pavilions, piers, sea walls and groves of palm trees. The two miles of coastline stretch from the Ala Wai Yacht Harbor to the Diamond Head Crater. This hike follows the Waikiki coastline through several beaches to Kapiolani Park, a grassy oasis under the cliffs of Diamond Head. The expansive park includes walking, jogging and biking paths.

Driving directions: Waikiki Beach and Kapiolani Park are accessible on foot from anywhere in Waikiki. If you are staying in Waikiki, a car is not necessary. This hike begins at the west end by the Hilton Hawaiian Village, east of the Ala Wai Yacht Harbor.

Hiking directions: You may begin the hike from any point along the Waikiki beachfront. This hike starts at the northwest end of Waikiki on Duke Kahanamoku Beach. From the oceanfront boardwalk fronting the Hilton Hawaiian Village, head southeast along Fort DeRussy Beach Park, a grassy, palm-lined park. The walkway ends at the Waikiki Shores. Follow the white sand of Gray's Beach in front of the hotel, and cross the footbridge over an ocean inlet, returning to the sand. Pick up the paved boardwalk again at the Sheraton Waikiki, and continue to the pink Royal Hawaiian Hotel. Return to the sandy beach, and either beachcomb past the umbrellas and water sport rentals, or take the beach access inland to Kalakaua Avenue. Both routes rejoin a short distance ahead at Kuhio Beach Park. Pass the black lava rock ocean barrier extending to Kapahulu Avenue. The walkway passes Queen's Beach and enters Kapiolani Park. Take the right fork, following the oceanfront esplanade through a Marine Conservation Area, passing the Waikiki Aquarium, the War Memorial and Sans Souci Beach. The beach is backed by the expansive green lawn and scattered trees of Kapiolani Park. To hike further, loop through the grassy expanse of the park along the base of Diamond Head Crater. Return back along the shoreline.

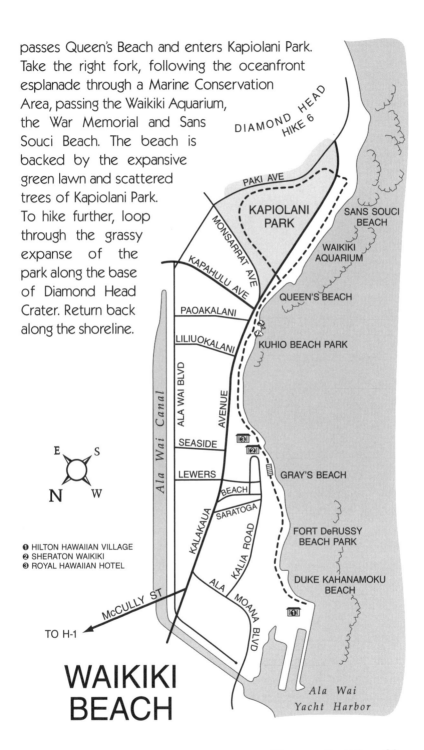

DIAMOND HEAD
HIKE 6

PAKI AVE

KAPIOLANI
PARK

SANS SOUCI
BEACH

WAIKIKI
AQUARIUM

MONSARRAT AVE

KAPAHULU AVE

QUEEN'S BEACH

PAOAKALANI

LILIUOKALANI

KUHIO BEACH PARK

Ala Wai Canal

ALA WAI BLVD

AVENUE

SEASIDE

LEWERS

GRAY'S BEACH

BEACH

SARATOGA

KALAKAUA

FORT DeRUSSY
BEACH PARK

KALIA ROAD

DUKE KAHANAMOKU
BEACH

ALA

MOANA BLVD

E
S
N
W

❶ HILTON HAWAIIAN VILLAGE
❷ SHERATON WAIKIKI
❸ ROYAL HAWAIIAN HOTEL

McCULLY ST

TO H-1

WAIKIKI
BEACH

Ala Wai
Yacht Harbor

Hike 8
Ala Wai Canal

Hiking distance: 3 miles round trip
Hiking time: 1.5 hours
Elevation gain: Level
Maps: U.S.G.S. Honolulu
　　　　Oahu Reference Maps: Honolulu/Oahu South Shore

Summary of hike: Ala Wai Canal, built in the 1920s, is a 1.5-mile waterway forming the inland boundary of Waikiki. A paved walkway borders the canal, stretching along the backside of Waikiki parallel to the ocean. This scenic tree-lined area is popular with walkers, joggers, kayakers, canoeists and catamaran teams. Swarming hoards of fish gather along the canal's shoreline, begging to be fed. The canal begins at the Ala Wai Harbor and extends to within a few blocks of Kapiolani Park and Diamond Head.

Driving directions: The Ala Wai Canal in Waikiki parallels the coastline about three blocks inland. If you are staying in Waikiki, a car is not necessary. Walk inland a few blocks to the canal.

Hiking directions: From Waikiki, head inland to the canal. Take the palm-lined walkway in either direction along the southwest banks of the canal. To the right, heading southeast, the paved path leads towards Diamond Head and Kapiolani Park. Taking the walkway to the left, the walking path leads to the Ala Wai Yacht Harbor on the northwest end of Waikiki, adjacent to Ala Moana Park (Hike 9). Along the way, the path crosses the intersection of Ala Wai Boulevard at McCully Street and at Kalakaua Avenue. To make a short loop on the other side of the canal, cross the bridge over the canal at Ala Moana Boulevard. Bear right on the Ala Wai Promenade along the north bank of the canal. Take the shady promenade back to Kalakaua Avenue. Cross the bridge over the canal to complete the loop. Return to the left, following the same route.

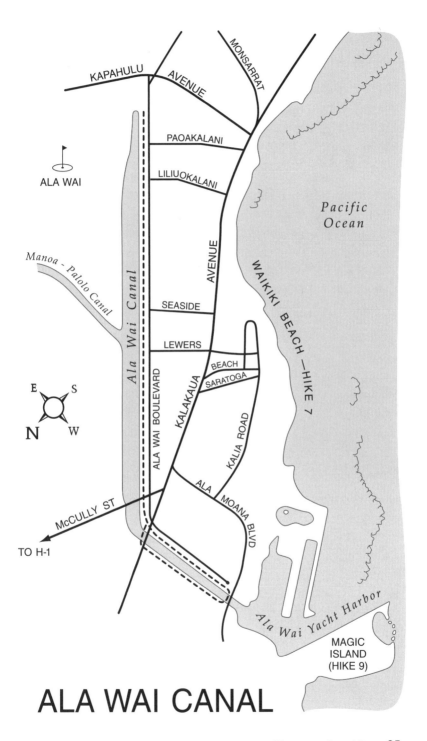

KAPAHULU AVENUE

MONSARRAT

ALA WAI

PAOAKALANI

LILIUOKALANI

Pacific Ocean

Manoa - Palolo Canal

AVENUE

Ala Wai Canal

SEASIDE

LEWERS

WAIKIKI BEACH —HIKE 7

BEACH

SARATOGA

KALAKAUA

ALA WAI BOULEVARD

KALIA ROAD

E S
N W

McCULLY ST

ALA MOANA BLVD

TO H-1

Ala Wai Yacht Harbor

MAGIC ISLAND (HIKE 9)

ALA WAI CANAL

Hike 9
Ala Moana Beach Park and Magic Island

Hiking distance: 2.2 miles round trip
Hiking time: 1 hour
Elevation gain: Level
Maps: U.S.G.S. Honolulu
        Oahu Reference Maps: Honolulu/Oahu South Shore

Summary of hike: Ala Moana Beach Park, within walking distance from downtown Waikiki, is a large and diverse park. The 76-acre park borders the Ala Wai Harbor and includes a huge grassy picnic area dotted with trees, several golden sand beaches, a lagoon, walking paths and a manmade peninsula and rocky point called Magic Island.

Driving directions: Ala Moana Park is in Honolulu at the west edge of Waikiki, across from the Ala Moana Shopping Center on Ala Moana Boulevard. The route can be walked, or the Ala Moana Shopping Center shuttle bus winds through Waikiki every 15 minutes, ending at the shopping center. If driving, take Ala Moana Boulevard west (towards the airport) less than one mile to Ala Moana Park Drive. Turn left and drive through the park to the parking lot on the left, or park alongside the harbor.

Hiking directions: Follow the palm-lined boardwalk along the Ala Wai Harbor channel. At the end of the grassy park area, continue south past the sandy beach along the breakwater to the point. Bear left around Magic Island, a calm swimming area with a barrier reef. Continue around the peninsula to the white sand of Ala Moana Beach. From here are several walking options. The path continues west across the large tree-lined park for 0.7 miles. At the west end of the park, a path extends into Kewalo Basin Park on a triangular peninsula. Other paths meander through the park to the lagoon and along the waterway. Choose your own route.

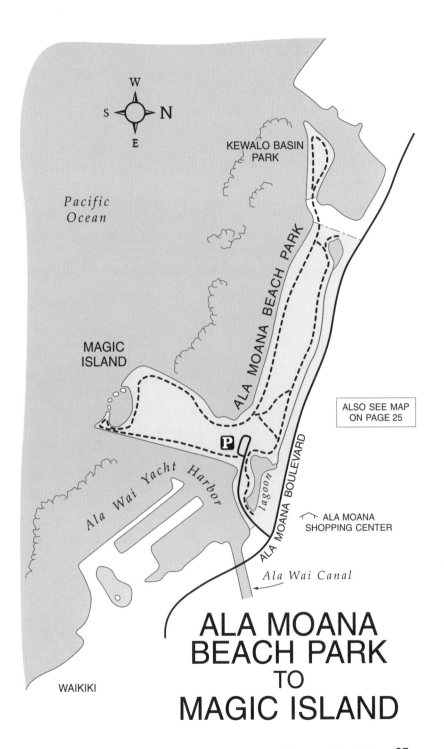

KEWALO BASIN PARK

Pacific Ocean

MAGIC ISLAND

ALA MOANA BEACH PARK

ALSO SEE MAP ON PAGE 25

Ala Wai Yacht Harbor

P

lagoon

ALA MOANA BOULEVARD

ALA MOANA SHOPPING CENTER

Ala Wai Canal

WAIKIKI

ALA MOANA BEACH PARK TO MAGIC ISLAND

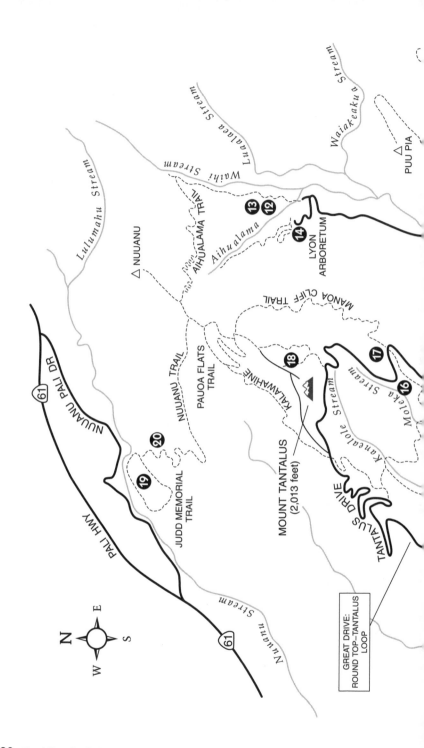

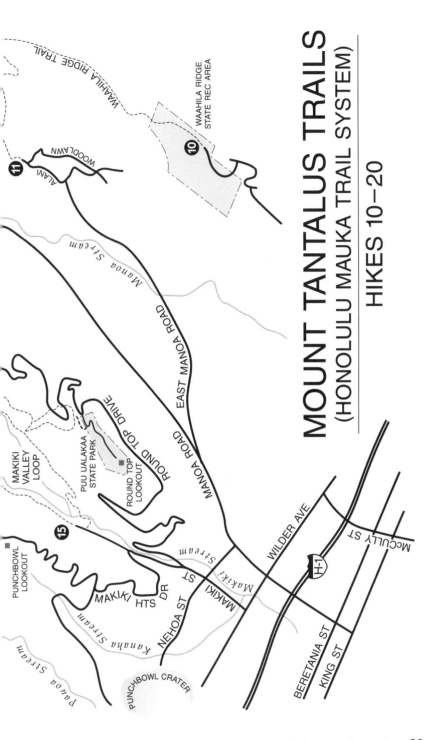

MOUNT TANTALUS TRAILS
(HONOLULU MAUKA TRAIL SYSTEM)

HIKES 10–20

Hike 10
Waahila Ridge Trail

Hiking distance: 3.5 miles round trip
Hiking time: 2 hours
Elevation gain: 1,000 feet
Maps: U.S.G.S. Honolulu
Oahu Reference Maps: Honolulu/Oahu South Shore
Honolulu Mauka Trail System Map

Summary of hike: The Waahila Ridge Trail is a forested path the follows the knife-edged spine of this mountain ridge, providing breathtaking panoramas of Manoa Valley, Palolo Valley, Waikiki and Diamond Head. The ridge route drops and climbs over numerous saddles and knobs, including a few steep and narrow spots. The trail passes through groves of Norfolk Island pine, guava, ironwood, koa and ohia trees.

Driving directions: From Waikiki, take McCully Street to Kapiolani Boulevard. Turn right and drive 1.4 miles to St. Louis Drive. Turn left and follow the winding St Louis Drive 2.3 miles to Bertram Street. Turn right on Bertram Street, and continue a short distance to Peter Street. Turn left on Peter Street, and drive 0.3 miles to Ruth Place. Turn left and enter Waahila Ridge State Recreation Area. The parking lot is 0.3 miles ahead.

Hiking directions: Begin at the far end of the parking lot. Several paths pass the picnic tables and continue through Norfolk Island pines. The paths converge and follow the ridge to the first plateau by power poles and a junction at 0.3 miles. Take the right fork downhill, passing many spur trails. Whenever you have a trail choice, stay on the ridge, contouring up and down the spine. The trail reaches a saddle and a junction at 1.7 miles. The wider Kolowalu Trail curves to the left and descends from the head of the valley down a narrow ridge, connecting with the Puu Pia Trail (Hike 11) in the valley below. The right fork follows the ridge to Mt. Olympus but enters the restricted watershed area en route. Return along the same route.

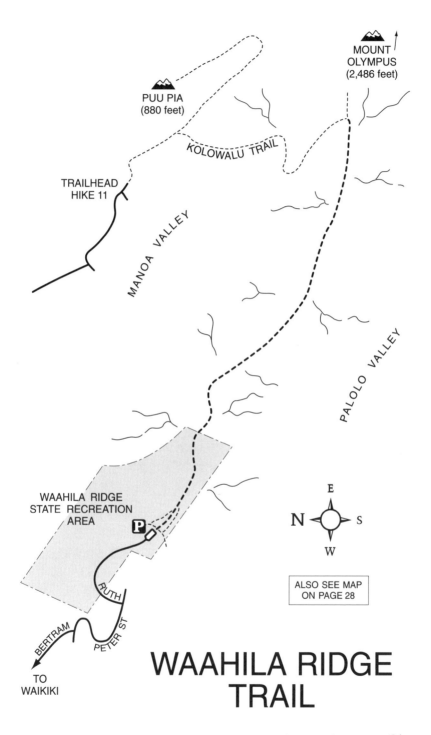

PUU PIA
(880 feet)

MOUNT
OLYMPUS
(2,486 feet)

KOLOWALU TRAIL

TRAILHEAD
HIKE 11

MANOA VALLEY

PALOLO VALLEY

WAAHILA RIDGE
STATE RECREATION
AREA

P

RUTH

BERTRAM

PETER ST

TO
WAIKIKI

E

N ⊕ S

W

ALSO SEE MAP
ON PAGE 28

WAAHILA RIDGE
TRAIL

Hike 11
Puu Pia Trail

Hiking distance: 1.8 miles round trip
Hiking time: 1 hour
Elevation gain: 500 feet
Maps: U.S.G.S. Honolulu
Oahu Reference Maps: Honolulu/Oahu South Shore
Honolulu Mauka Trail System map

Summary of hike: Puu Pia is an 880-foot mountain that sits in a scenic cirque in Manoa Valley, surrounded by the Honolulu Watershed Forest Reserve. At the summit are sweeping panoramic vistas—from the steep rainforests of the Koolau Range to Waikiki, the blue Pacific and the volcanic profile of Diamond Head. The trail follows a forested path, climbs the valley to a ridge and follows the ridge to the summit of Puu Pia.

Driving directions: From Waikiki, take McCully Street to Wilder Avenue at the first traffic light after crossing over H-1. Turn left on Wilder Avenue, and drive 0.4 to Punahou Street. Turn right on Punahou Street, which becomes Manoa Road, and drive 0.6 miles to a road split. Take the right fork onto East Manoa Road. Continue 1.8 miles to a T-junction at Alani Drive. Turn left and go 0.2 miles to a junction with Woodland Drive. Park along the side of the road near the junction.

Hiking directions: The trail begins as an extension of Alani Drive. Head north on the multi-home driveway at 3689 Alani Drive to the signed trailhead. Enter the jungle path and head uphill 0.2 miles to a trail junction and shelter on a grassy flat. The Kolowalu Trail bears right and climbs a steep narrow ridge, connecting with the Waahila Ridge Trail (Hike 10). Stay left on the Puu Pia Trail, steadily climbing up the damp, shady valley along the right side of a streambed. At 0.6 miles, cross the gully on a horseshoe bend to the left. Steeply climb up the exposed ridge—with awesome views in all directions—to the Puu Pia summit. After savoring the views, return along the same path.

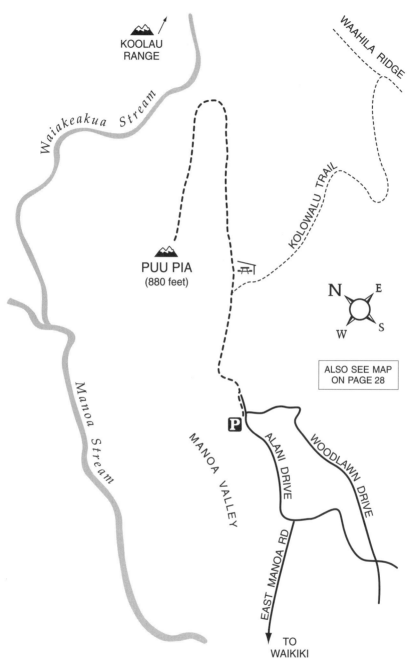

KOOLAU RANGE

Waiakeakua Stream

PUU PIA
(880 feet)

Manoa Stream

KOLOWALU TRAIL

WAAHILA RIDGE

N E
W S

ALSO SEE MAP
ON PAGE 28

P

MANOA VALLEY

ALANI DRIVE

WOODLAWN DRIVE

EAST MANOA RD

TO
WAIKIKI

PUU PIA TRAIL

Hike 12
Manoa Falls

Hiking distance: 1.6 miles round trip
Hiking time: 1 hour
Elevation gain: 500 feet
Maps: U.S.G.S. Honolulu
Oahu Reference Maps: Honolulu/Oahu South Shore
Honolulu Mauka Trail System map

Summary of hike: Manoa Falls is a towering 100-foot cataract in the beautiful rainforest behind Waikiki. A white ribbon of water cascades off the fern-faced cliffs, fronted by a shallow rock-lined pool. The Manoa Falls Trail parallels Waihi Stream through the forest reserve to the falls. The path is dense with vegetation, including wild ginger, guava and giant ferns. A mosaic of sinuous tree roots lay across the muddy, and sometimes slippery, jungle path.

Driving directions: From Waikiki, take McCully Street to Wilder Avenue at the first traffic light after crossing over H-1. Turn left on Wilder Avenue and drive 0.4 to Punahou Street. Turn right on Punahou Street, which becomes Manoa Road, and drive 0.6 miles to a road split. Take the left fork, staying on Manoa Road to a 5-way junction at 1 mile. Curve to the right, continuing on Manoa Road past the Paradise Park parking lot. The Manoa Falls Trail is a short distance past this parking lot. Park on the short trailhead road before the main road curves sharply to the left towards Lyon Arboretum.

Hiking directions: Walk past the end of the road and follow the footpath slightly uphill. Cross a footbridge over Aihualama Stream. Veer left on the muddy main trail, crossing a network of tangled roots and trees draped with vines along the west bank of Waihi Stream. As you near Manoa Falls, the valley narrows and the trail steepens. Thirty yards before the falls, Aihualama Trail (Hike 13) branches sharply to the left, connecting with the Mount Tantalus trails. (A few feet up the Aihualama

Trail is a great overview of the falls and pool.) Continue on the main trail to the base of Manoa Falls at the pool. Return on the same route.

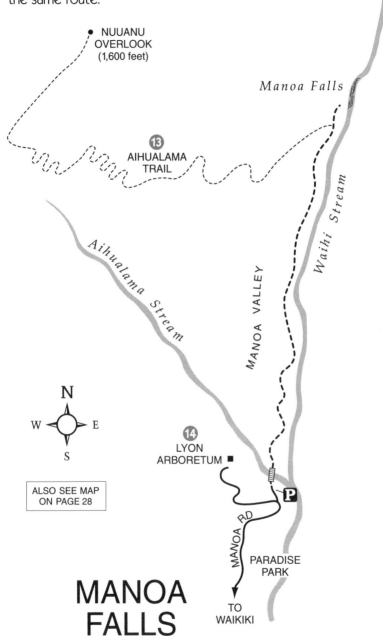

● NUUANU
OVERLOOK
(1,600 feet)

Manoa Falls

13
AIHUALAMA
TRAIL

Waihi Stream

Aihualama Stream

MANOA VALLEY

N
W ◄—●—► E
S

14
LYON
ARBORETUM ■

ALSO SEE MAP
ON PAGE 28

P

MANOA RD

PARADISE
PARK

MANOA
FALLS

TO
WAIKIKI

Hike 13
Aihualama Trail to Nuuanu Overlook

Hiking distance: 5.6 miles round trip
Hiking time: 3 hours
Elevation gain: 1,100 feet
Maps: U.S.G.S. Honolulu
      Oahu Reference Maps: Honolulu/Oahu South Shore
      Honolulu Mauka Trail System map

Summary of hike: The Aihualama Trail begins at Manoa Falls (Hike 12), skirts the upper end of Manoa Valley, then heads steeply up to Pauoa Flats and a stunning overlook. The route passes through groves of bamboo, koa, eucalyptus and enormous banyan trees. The are great views across the valley to Waikiki and Diamond Head. From the Nuuanu Overlook at the trail's end are panoramic vistas overlooking the Nuuanu Valley and the rugged Koolau Mountains.

Driving directions: From Waikiki, take McCully Street to Wilder Avenue at the first traffic light after crossing over H-1. Turn left on Wilder Avenue and drive 0.4 to Punahou Street. Turn right on Punahou Street, which becomes Manoa Road, and drive 0.6 miles to a road split. Take the left fork, staying on Manoa Road to a 5-way junction at 1 mile. Curve to the right, continuing on Manoa Road past the Paradise Park parking lot. The Manoa Falls Trail is a short distance past this parking lot. Park on the short trailhead road before the main road curves sharply to the left towards Lyon Arboretum.

Hiking directions: Follow the hiking directions to Manoa Falls—Hike 12. Just before reaching the waterfall and pool is a junction on the left with the Aihualama Trail. Bear left and head uphill a short distance to a great overview of Manoa Falls and pool. Follow the contours of the hillside, crossing several gullies to views overlooking Manoa Valley, Waahila Ridge and Waikiki. Ascend fourteen sharp switchbacks out of Manoa Valley to a ridge in a large bamboo forest. At the ridge the

Aihualama Trail ends at a signed junction with the Puu Ohia Trail on Pauoa Flats. Take the right fork 0.7 miles through a maze of exposed tree roots, bamboo and eucalyptus groves to the end of the trail at the Nuuanu Overlook. Return on the same trail.

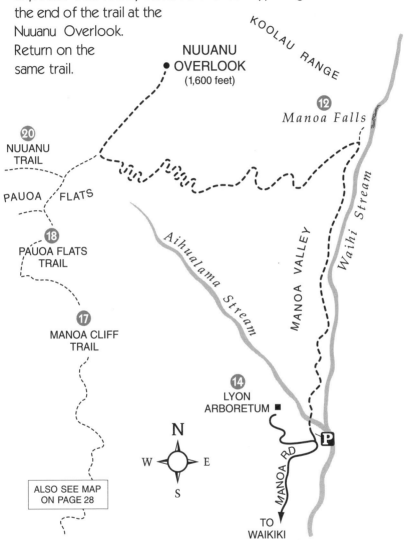

AIHUALAMA TRAIL TO NUUANU OVERLOOK

Hike 14
Lyon Arboretum
3860 Manoa Road
Open Monday—Saturday · 9 a.m.—3 p.m.

Hiking distance: 1.5 miles round trip
Hiking time: 1 hour
Elevation gain: 200 feet
Maps: U.S.G.S. Honolulu
Oahu Reference Maps: Honolulu/Oahu South Shore
Harold L. Lyon Arboretum guide

Summary of hike: Lyon Arboretum is a botanical research facility backed against the Koolau Mountains in the lush Manoa Valley. The 194-acre facility and tropical garden has a vast collection of rare, endangered and exotic tropical plants with descriptions of their uses, such as food, medicine, clothing, building materials and musical instruments. Part of the University of Hawaii, this facility is instrumental in conservation biology, horticulture and ethnobotany research. The arboretum has two short hikes. A half-mile hike leads to Inspiration Point overlooking the upper Manoa Valley. A one-mile hike follows a service road parallel to Aihualama Stream, weaving through exotic palm, macadamia, ginger, banyan trees and blooming orchids. A guide is available at the registration center.

Driving directions: From Waikiki, take McCully Street to Wilder Avenue at the first traffic light after crossing over H-1. Turn left on Wilder Avenue and drive 0.4 to Punahou Street. Turn right on Punahou Street, which becomes Manoa Road, and drive 0.6 miles to a road split. Take the left fork, staying on Manoa Road to a 5-way junction at 1 mile. Curve to the right, continuing on Manoa Road past the Paradise Park parking lot. Continue a half mile further, curving sharply to the left to the arboretum at the end of the road.

Hiking directions: The half mile path to Inspiration Point begins on the stone path at the upper west end of the parking area. Follow the path gently uphill, wandering through the beautiful gardens as the path fades in and out. Inspiration Point is at the top of the grassy hillside.

The one-mile hike also begins at the west end of the parking area. Take the service road past the gate, and follow the winding road past the Hawaiian Ethnobotanical Garden and a research area. Disregard the intersecting side paths, staying on the road past the lush gardens and shade trees. As the road narrows to a walking track, side paths on the right lead to small pools and trickling water at Aihualama Stream. Return along the same route.

HAWAIIAN SECTION

INSPIRATION POINT

Aihualama Stream

W N
S
E

ALSO SEE MAP ON PAGE 28

HAWAIIAN ETHNOBOTANICAL GARDEN

RECEPTION CENTER AND GIFT SHOP

P

TO MANOA FALLS (HIKE 12)

MANOA ROAD

TO WAIKIKI

Waihi Stream

LYON ARBORETUM

Hike 15
Makiki Valley Loop

Hiking distance: 2 miles round trip
Hiking time: 1 hour
Elevation gain: 550 feet
Maps: U.S.G.S. Honolulu
  Oahu Reference Maps: Honolulu/Oahu South Shore
  Honolulu Mauka Trail System Maps

Summary of hike: The Makiki Valley Loop is located in the lush tropical forest of Makiki Valley. The paths loops on three trails through eucalyptus and bamboo groves up, across and back down the valley. There are several stream crossings and scenic views of Honolulu and the Manoa Valley.

Driving directions: From Waikiki, take McCully Street to Wilder Avenue at the first traffic light after crossing over H-1. Turn left on Wilder Avenue, and drive 0.6 miles to Makiki Street. Turn right and go 0.3 miles to a road fork at the triangular-shaped Archie Baker Park. Curve to the left and continue 0.4 miles to a sharp, curving switchback to the left. Do not take the switchback. Instead, go straight (north) onto the smaller road which leads into Makiki Valley. Park on the side of the road by the park, just below the Hawaii Nature Center.

Hiking directions: From the end of the road, pass the Hawaii Nature Center and the forestry baseyard to the trail-head. Take the signed Kanealole Trail up the Makiki Valley. Walk through the shady forest along the west side of Kanealole Stream. The trail ends at 0.7 miles by a signed junction with the Makiki Valley Trail. Bear right, crossing several branches of Kanealole Stream. Continue across the Makiki Valley, contouring around the ridges and gullies to Moleka Stream. Cross a foot-bridge over the stream to a posted four-way junction with the Maunalaha and Ualakaa Trails. Take the Maunalaha Trail to the right, following the east ridge of the valley through oak, guava and eucalyptus groves. Slowly descend to Kanealole Stream.

Wind through a forest of Norfolk Island and Cook pines, and cross a footbridge over the stream, returning to the trailhead at the nature center.

Kanealole Stream

MAKIKI VALLEY TRAIL

MOLEKA TRAIL

Kanealole Stream

MAKIKI VALLEY

KANEALOLE TRAIL

Moleka Stream

MOLEKA TRAIL

🔟16

UALAKAA TRAIL

MAUNALAHA TRAIL

Ⓟ

HAWAII NATURE CENTER

N
W — E
S

ALSO SEE MAP ON PAGE 28

MAKIKI HTS DR

ROUND TOP DR

TO WAIKIKI

MAKIKI VALLEY LOOP

Hike 16
Moleka and Ualakaa Trails

Hiking distance: 2 miles round trip
Hiking time: 1 hour
Elevation gain: 350 feet
Maps: U.S.G.S. Honolulu
Honolulu Mauka Trail System Map
Oahu Reference Maps: Honolulu/Oahu South Shore

Summary of hike: The Moleka and Ualakaa Trails were established by the Sierra Club in 1979 and 1980. The two trails traverse the hillside through the upper east edge of Makiki Valley with panoramic views down the valley. Both paths wind past large banyan trees and through forests of bamboo, ginger, ti and lobster claw. The looping Ualakaa Trail connects the Makiki Valley Trail (Hike 15) with Puu Ualakaa State Park.

Driving directions: From Waikiki, take McCully Street to Wilder Avenue at the first traffic light after crossing over H-1. Turn left on Wilder Avenue and drive 0.6 miles to Makiki Street. Turn right and go 0.3 miles to a road fork at the triangular-shaped Archie Baker Park. Curve to the right onto Round Top Drive, and continue 4.3 miles up the curving road to the signed trailhead parking spaces on the left.

Hiking directions: Head down the well-defined Moleka Trail through the dense forest. Traverse the hillside, overlooking the Makiki Valley and the ocean below, to a T-junction at 0.7 miles. Begin the loop to the right, reaching a posted four-way junction with the Makiki Valley, Maunalaha and Ualakaa Trails. Take the Ualakaa Trail to the left, winding through the forest. The path crosses Round Top Drive and reenters the forest directly across the road. Continue through the shade of the jungle to a second crossing of Round Top Drive. Walk up the road about 50 yards and reenter the dense forest again. Pass huge banyan trees to the T-junction, completing the loop. Return to the right on the Moleka Trail.

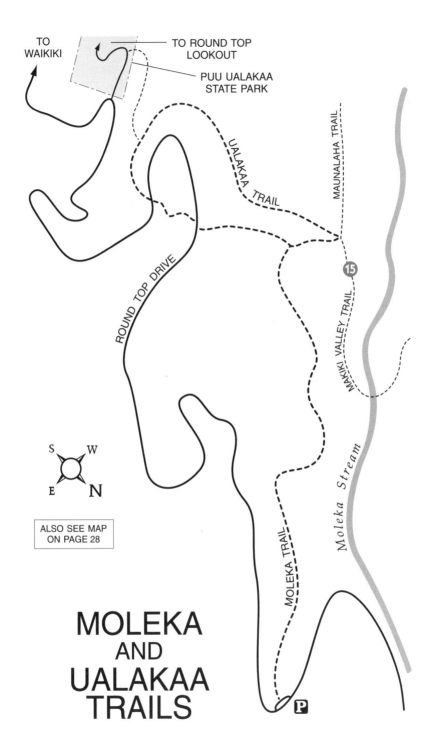

TO WAIKIKI

TO ROUND TOP LOOKOUT

PUU UALAKAA STATE PARK

UALAKAA TRAIL

MAUNALAHA TRAIL

ROUND TOP DRIVE

MAKIKI VALLEY TRAIL

15

Moleka Stream

S W
E N

ALSO SEE MAP
ON PAGE 28

MOLEKA TRAIL

MOLEKA
AND
UALAKAA
TRAILS

P

Hike 17
Manoa Cliff—Kalawahine Loop

Hiking distance: 4.8 mile loop
Hiking time: 2.5 hours
Elevation gain: 900 feet
Maps: U.S.G.S. Honolulu
Oahu Reference Maps: Honolulu/Oahu South Shore
Honolulu Mauka Trail System map

Summary of hike: The Manoa Cliff and Kalawahine Trails loop around Tantalus Crater. The hike begins on the Manoa Cliff Trail at Round Top Drive and traverses a spectacular precipice on the west side of Manoa Valley. The Kalawahine Trail returns along the northwest flank of Tantalus on the forested cliffs above Pauoa Valley, exiting at Tantalus Drive. En route, there are great views of Manoa Valley, the Koolau Range, Pearl Harbor and Pearl City.

Driving directions: From Waikiki, take McCully Street to Wilder Avenue at the first traffic light after crossing over H-1. Turn left on Wilder Avenue, and drive 0.6 miles to Makiki Street. Turn right and go 0.3 miles to a road fork at the triangular-shaped Archie Baker Park. Curve to the right onto Round Top Drive, and continue 4.3 miles up the curving road to the signed Moleka Trail parking spaces on the left.

Hiking directions: The signed Manoa Cliff Trail begins across the road to the north. Enter the lush forest, gaining gradual but steady elevation. The well-defined path climbs some steps and winds up the mountain. Follow the edge of the cliff past a number of vista points overlooking Manoa Valley to the east. Descend to a signed junction with the Puu Ohia Trail at 1.4 miles. Stay on the Manoa Cliff Trail straight ahead on the right fork, gradually descending 0.2 miles to a junction and trail map with the Pauoa Flats Trail on the right. Stay left through the ginger and fern-lined path, heading down switchbacks to a junction with the Kalawahine Trail a half mile ahead. Bear left, curving along the contours of the mountainside above Pauoa Valley for 1.1 mile. Reach the trail's end at Tantalus Drive. Follow the road 1.5 miles to the left (east) back to the trailhead.

Note: The maps refer to the entire trail as Manoa Cliff but the signage along the route designates the last portion as the Kalawahine Trail.

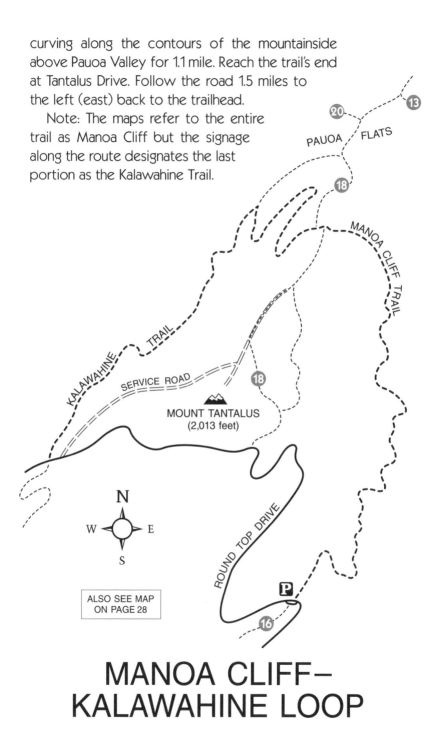

MANOA CLIFF– KALAWAHINE LOOP

Hike 18
Puu Ohia—Pauoa Flats Loop

Hiking distance: 3 miles round trip
Hiking time: 1.5 hours
Elevation gain: 400 feet
Maps: U.S.G.S. Honolulu
      Oahu Reference Maps: Honolulu/Oahu South Shore
      Honolulu Mauka Trail System map

Summary of hike: The Puu Ohia Trail climbs over the top of Tantalus Crater through a lush rainforest with groves of guava, ginger, eucalyptus, Norfolk Island pine and bamboo. The trail loops around Pauoa Flats to magnificent vistas above Pauoa, Nuuanu and Manoa Valleys.

Driving directions: From Waikiki, take McCully Street to Wilder Avenue at the first traffic light after crossing over H-1. Turn left on Wilder Avenue, and drive 0.6 miles to Makiki Street. Turn right and go 0.3 miles to a road fork at the triangular-shaped Archie Baker Park. Curve to the right onto Round Top Drive, and continue 5.3 miles up the curving road to the signed trailhead parking lot on the left at the top of the road loop.

Hiking directions: Cross the road to the signed trail, and enter the jungle, heading sharply uphill. Wind through a thick bamboo forest, passing two short side paths on the right that lead to overlooks of the Tantalus (Puu Ohia) Crater. The main trail continues to a junction with a paved service road. Take the road to the right for a quarter mile to the telephone relay station. Pick up the signed footpath on the left, and descend into another bamboo forest. Curve right to a signed T-junction with the Manoa Cliff Trail. Bear left 0.2 miles downhill to a junction and trail map. Begin the loop to the left on the Manoa Cliff Trail, reaching a junction with the Kalawahine Trail (Hike 17). Take the right fork through the shady forest canopy, crossing a mosaic of exposed roots to Pauoa Flats and a posted junction. Take the right fork on the Pauoa Flats Trail through eucalyptus groves. Head steeply up the side of Tantalus back to the Manoa Cliff Trail, completing the loop. Bear left a short distance back to the Puu Ohia Trail. Retrace your steps to the right.

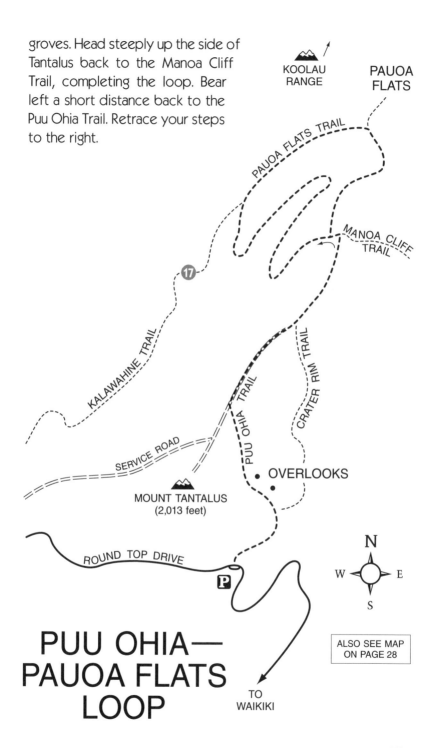

KOOLAU RANGE

PAUOA FLATS

PAUOA FLATS TRAIL

MANOA CLIFF TRAIL

17

KALAWAHINE TRAIL

CRATER RIM TRAIL

PUU OHIA TRAIL

SERVICE ROAD

MOUNT TANTALUS
(2,013 feet)

OVERLOOKS

ROUND TOP DRIVE

P

N
W E
S

PUU OHIA— PAUOA FLATS LOOP

ALSO SEE MAP
ON PAGE 28

TO
WAIKIKI

Hike 19
Judd Memorial Trail
to Jackass Ginger Pool

Hiking distance: 1 mile loop
Hiking time: 1 hour
Elevation gain: 200 feet
Maps: U.S.G.S. Honolulu
Oahu Reference Maps: Honolulu/Oahu South Shore
Honolulu Mauka Trail System map

Summary of hike: The Judd Memorial Trail is a short loop hike in the Nuuanu Valley. The path crosses the Nuuanu Stream and traverses the north-facing hillside through bamboo, eucalyptus and Norfolk Island pine groves. A side path leads down to Jackass Ginger Pool, a large circular pool with a 10-foot waterfall cascading over rocks into the pool.

Driving directions: From Waikiki, take H-1 west 1.5 miles to the Pali Highway (61) north. Drive 2.5 miles on the Pali Highway to the Nuuanu Pali Drive exit. Take the turnoff to the right, and stay on Nuuanu Pali Drive for one mile to the signed trailhead parking lot on the right. If the lot is closed, park along the side of the road.

Hiking directions: Descend towards Nuuanu Stream. Rock-hop across the stream to a junction at the signed Judd Trail. Begin the loop on the left fork through a giant bamboo grove. The serpentine path gains elevation, traversing the hillside above the stream through eucalyptus and Norfolk Island pines. Descend and cross a small gully to a signed trail with the Nuuanu Trail on the left (Hike 20). Stay to the right on the Judd Trail, and drop back down the hill. As you reach a residential area, the path curves right and begins returning high above and parallel to Nuuanu Stream. Watch for a metal stake marking a side path on the left. Take this short, steep side path 25 yards to Jackass Ginger Pool. After enjoying the pool, return to the Judd Trail and bear left. Additional side paths on the left lead down to smaller pools with cascades and waterfalls. The main trail slopes gradually down to Nuuanu Stream, completing the loop. Before recrossing the stream to the trailhead, follow the watercourse about 10 yards upstream to another waterfall.

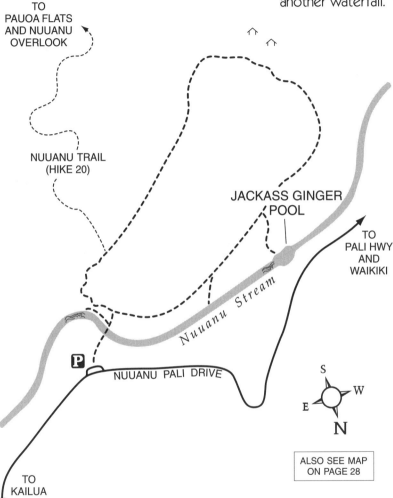

JUDD MEMORIAL TRAIL
TO
JACKASS GINGER POOL

Hike 20
Nuuanu Trail to Nuuanu Overlook

Hiking distance: 5.6 miles round trip
Hiking time: 3 hours
Elevation gain: 1,000 feet
Maps: U.S.G.S. Honolulu
Oahu Reference Maps: Honolulu/Oahu South Shore
Honolulu Mauka Trail System map

Summary of hike: The Nuuanu Trail begins in Nuuanu Valley on the Judd Memorial Trail (Hike 19) and heads up to Nuuanu Overlook at 1,600 feet. The trail crosses Nuuanu Stream and climbs through lush tropical groves of bamboo, Norfolk Island pines, eucalyptus and a maze of muddy tree roots. From the overlook are sweeping views of the Waianae Range, Honolulu, Nuuanu Valley and the rugged Koolau Mountains.

Driving directions: Follow the driving directions for Hike 19.

Hiking directions: Descend towards Nuuanu Stream. Rock-hop across the stream to a signed junction with the Judd Trail. Take the left fork through a bamboo grove, and ascend the lush hillside on the serpentine path. Traverse the hillside through a Norfolk Island pine forest above the Nuuanu Stream. Cross a small gully to a signed junction. The right fork stays on the Judd Trail (Hike 19). Take the Nuuanu Trail to the left, winding up the northwest flank of Tantalus. Steep switchbacks climb the west wall of Nuuanu Valley through ironwood, palm and eucalyptus groves, with views across the Pauoa Valley to the city below. Cross a trickling stream as the shaded trail levels out at a signed junction on Pauoa Flats at 2 miles. The right fork leads to Mount Tantalus. Take the Pauoa Flats Trail to the left through a mosaic of tangled tree roots, passing the Aihualama Trail on the right (Hike 13). Stay on the Pauoa Flats Trail 0.7 miles to a small clearing at the Nuuanu Overlook. Return on the same trail.

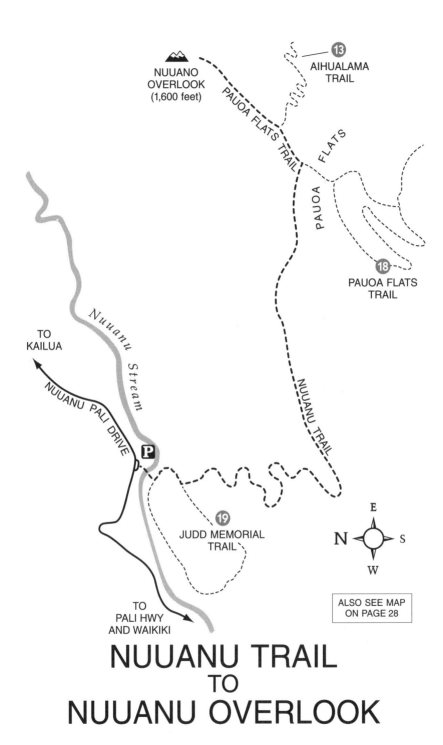

NUUANO
OVERLOOK
(1,600 feet)

13 AIHUALAMA
TRAIL

PAUOA FLATS TRAIL

PAUOA FLATS

PAUOA

18 PAUOA FLATS
TRAIL

Nuuanu Stream

TO
KAILUA

NUUANU PALI DRIVE

P

NUUANU TRAIL

19 JUDD MEMORIAL
TRAIL

E
N
W S

TO
PALI HWY
AND WAIKIKI

ALSO SEE MAP
ON PAGE 28

NUUANU TRAIL
TO
NUUANU OVERLOOK

Hike 21
Foster Botanical Garden
50 North Vineyard Boulevard
Open daily · 9 a.m.—4 p.m.

Hiking distance: .5 to 1 mile round trip
Hiking time: 1 hour
Elevation gain: Level
Maps: U.S.G.S. Honolulu
Foster Botanical Garden map

Summary of hike: Foster Botanical Gardens, listed on the National Register of Historic Places, is a living museum dating back to 1853. This 14-acre verdant garden is Hawaii's oldest botanical garden and is a pastoral oasis surrounded by the hectic downtown business district of Honolulu. The gardens include a wide cross section of tropical plant life, including two orchid displays; herb and spice gardens; and palm, ginger, coffee, chocolate, cannonball and banyan trees. There are rare, endangered plants from both Hawaii and all over the world. A guide is available at the gift shop and entrance kiosk.

Driving directions: From Waikiki, take McCully Street to Beretania Street, located just before crossing over H-1. Turn left and drive 2.3 miles to Nuuanu Avenue. Turn right and drive to Vineyard Boulevard at the second traffic light. Turn left on Vineyard Boulevard, and go one block to the botanic garden parking lot on the right.

Hiking directions: Upon entering the gardens, it is apparent that an exact hiking route is unnecessary. There are so many gardens and paths to explore that you will immediately be pulled towards your own interests. A few paths lead through tree-shaded areas to the numerous gardens. You may also wander across the grassy expanses to the seemingly endless garden displays.

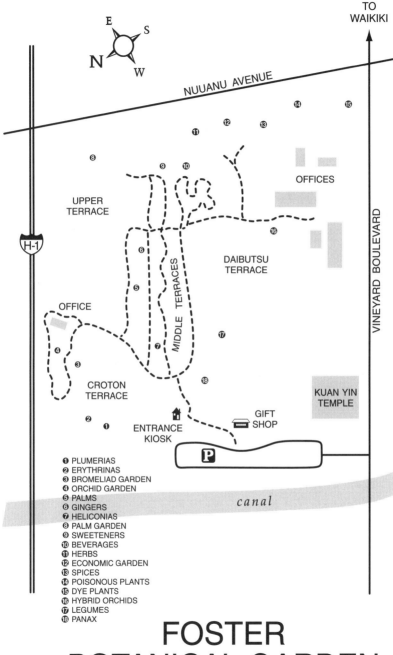

TO
WAIKIKI

NUUANU AVENUE

E
S
N
W

H-1

⑭ ⑮

⑪ ⑫ ⑬

OFFICES

⑧

⑨ ⑩

UPPER
TERRACE

⑯

⑥

DAIBUTSU
TERRACE

⑤

MIDDLE TERRACES

OFFICE

⑰

④

③

CROTON
TERRACE

⑱

② ①

ENTRANCE
KIOSK

GIFT
SHOP

KUAN YIN
TEMPLE

P

canal

VINEYARD BOULEVARD

❶ PLUMERIAS
❷ ERYTHRINAS
❸ BROMELIAD GARDEN
❹ ORCHID GARDEN
❺ PALMS
❻ GINGERS
❼ HELICONIAS
❽ PALM GARDEN
❾ SWEETENERS
❿ BEVERAGES
⓫ HERBS
⓬ ECONOMIC GARDEN
⓭ SPICES
⓮ POISONOUS PLANTS
⓯ DYE PLANTS
⓰ HYBRID ORCHIDS
⓱ LEGUMES
⓲ PANAX

FOSTER
BOTANICAL GARDEN

Hike 22
Alapena Pool and Falls

Hiking distance: 0.5 miles round trip
Hiking time: 15 minutes
Elevation gain: 50 feet
Maps: U.S.G.S. Honolulu
Oahu Reference Maps: Honolulu/Oahu South Shore

Summary of hike: Alapena Pool sits in a gorgeous jungle setting a short distance off the Pali Highway in Honolulu. Alapena Falls is a 15-foot cascade on Nuuanu Stream that tumbles into the deep pool. The short, unsigned path leads directly to the pool, which is popular with locals but relatively unknown as a tourist destination.

Driving directions: From Waikiki, take H-1 west 1.5 miles to the Pali Highway (61) north. Drive 1 mile north to the Wyllie Street exit. Loop around and return back towards Honolulu on the Pali Highway. Return 0.2 miles to the signed "Scenic Lookout" turnout on the right, overlooking a beautiful pagoda.

Hiking directions: After viewing the scenic lookout and pagoda, walk a hundred yards up the Pali Highway, away from Honolulu. Watch for a trail on the left at the end of the rock wall. Take the footpath into the shade of the lush tropical forest. A short distance ahead is an overlook of Alpena Falls cascading into the large pool. The path descends to the banks of the pool across from the waterfall. The path continues downstream to a few additional smaller waterfalls and pools. Return to your vehicle along the same route.

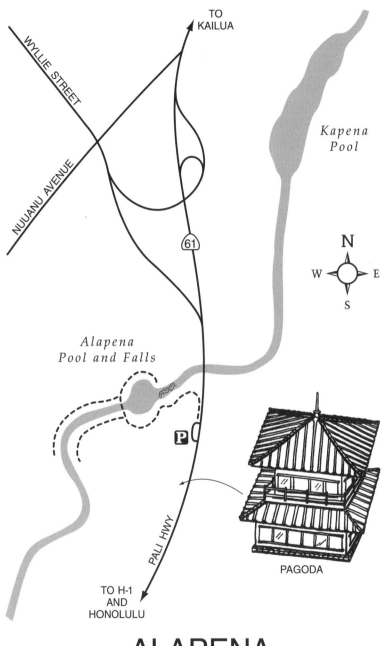

WYLLIE STREET

NUUANU AVENUE

TO
KAILUA

61

*Kapena
Pool*

N
W · E
S

*Alapena
Pool and Falls*

P

PALI HWY

PAGODA

TO H-1
AND
HONOLULU

ALAPENA
POOL AND FALLS

Hike 23
Old Pali Road and Pali Lookout

Hiking distance: 2 miles round trip
Hiking time: 1 hour
Elevation gain: 350 feet
Maps: U.S.G.S. Honolulu
  Oahu Reference Maps: Central Oahu/Windward Coast

Summary of hike: This hike heads downhill along an abandoned portion of the Old Pali Highway built in 1932. The area is lush with vegetation that is slowly taking over the road. The trail begins at the Pali Lookout on the summit of the Koolau Mountains. From the clifftop perch are sweeping vistas of Windward Oahu from an elevation of 1,200 feet. It overlooks the towns and bays of Kailua and Kaneohe. These spectacular, unobstructed views extend across the vertical ridges, tall forbidding peaks, and deep valleys of the sheer Pali cliffs to the coastal plain and ocean below. The lookout is often windy but the views are staggering.

Driving directions: From Waikiki, take H-1 west 1.5 miles to the Pali Highway (61) north. Drive 5.4 miles north to the signed Pali Lookout and Nuuanu Pali State Park exit on the right. Exit and continue 0.3 miles to the state park parking lot.

Hiking directions: Walk to the brink of the cliffs on the Pali Lookout platform. On each side of the lookout are paths that meet at the lower lookout level. Go to the right past a gate, and begin a gentle descent with lush cliffs on the right and the commanding views toward the sea and Kaneohe Bay on the left. As you near the Pali Highway, the wide old road narrows to a footpath that weaves between fallen boulders from the eroded cliffs above. This is the turnaround spot. Return along the same path.

To hike further, the trail continues, connecting with the Maunawili Demonstration Trail (Hike 24) 0.7 miles further.

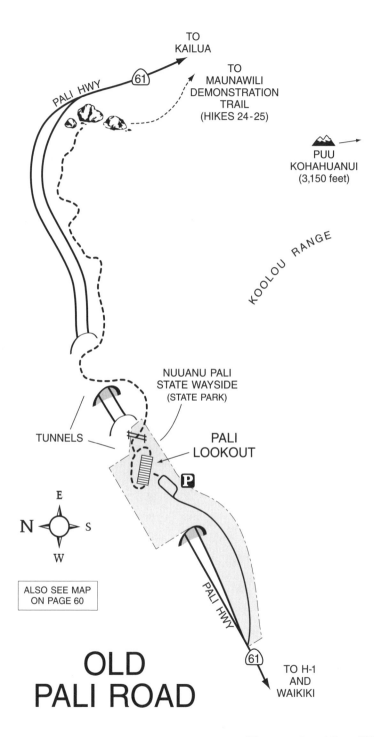

TO
KAILUA

TO
MAUNAWILI
DEMONSTRATION
TRAIL
(HIKES 24-25)

PALI HWY   61

PUU
KOHAHUANUI
(3,150 feet)

KOOLOU RANGE

NUUANU PALI
STATE WAYSIDE
(STATE PARK)

TUNNELS

PALI
LOOKOUT

P

E

N   S

W

ALSO SEE MAP
ON PAGE 60

PALI HWY

61

TO H-1
AND
WAIKIKI

OLD
PALI ROAD

Hike 24
Maunawili Demonstration Trail
West Trailhead from Nuuanu Pali Lookout

Hiking distance: 4 miles round trip
Hiking time: 2 hours
Elevation gain: 300 feet
Maps: U.S.G.S. Honolulu and Koko Head
       Oahu Reference Maps: Central Oahu/Windward Coast

map
next page

Summary of hike: The Maunawili Demonstration Trail is a well-defined tropical forest hike with scenic vistas across the windward side of the Koolau Range. The 9.3-mile trail connects the Nuuanu Pali Lookout with Waimanalo on the windward coast, circling around the three distinct peaks of Mount Olomana to the northeast. This hike follows the first two miles of the trail along the north wall of Maunawili Valley on the lush slopes of the Koolau Mountains. The hike can be combined with the trail from the Waimanalo trailhead (Hike 25) for a one-way shuttle hike.

Driving directions: From Waikiki, take H-1 west 1.5 miles to the Pali Highway (61) north. Drive 6.9 miles north, passing through two tunnels, to the signed "Scenic Point" turnout on the right. Park in the turnout.

Hiking directions: Walk back to the top of the turnout by the opening in the guard rail. Take the footpath past the trail sign into the lush tropical forest with an understory of ferns and jungle vines. Pass green, moss-covered rocks, following the contours of the mountain past a junction on the right to Nuuanu Pali State Wayside (Hike 23). Cross gullies and drainages with footbridges, boardwalks and numerous trickling streams. Pass a water tank on the right by an overlook of Kailua and the ocean. Zigzag down into the wet, lush gullies, then cross over ridges with vistas of the surrounding mountains. This up and down route of lush drainages and ridges with differing scenic views continues for miles. Choose your own turnaround spot.

Hike 25
Maunawili Demonstration Trail
East Trailhead from Waimanalo

Hiking distance: 2.6 miles round trip
Hiking time: 1.5 hours
Elevation gain: 450 feet
Maps: U.S.G.S. Koko Head
       Oahu Reference Maps: Central Oahu/Windward Coast

map
next page

Summary of hike: The Maunawili Demonstration Trail is a 9.3-mile trail from Waimanalo to Nuuanu Pali Lookout on the Pali Highway. This hike follows the first 1.3 miles of the trail from the east trailhead to the Aniani Nui Ridge, the south ridge descending from Mount Olomana. The hike can be combined with the trail from the Nuuanu Pali Lookout Trailhead (Hike 24) for a one-way shuttle hike. (For the shuttle hike, it is easier to begin from the Pali Highway and walk downhill.)

Driving directions: From Waikiki, take H–1 west 1.5 miles to the Pali Highway (61) north. Drive 9.5 miles north to the end of the Pali Highway in Kailua, where the Pali Highway crosses the Kalanianaole Highway (72) and becomes Kailua Road. Turn right on Highway 72, and drive 3.1 miles to Kumuhau Street on the right, just past the Olomana Golf Course. Turn right on Kumuhau Street, and go 1 mile to a T-junction with Waikupanaha Street. Turn right and continue 0.2 miles to the signed trailhead on the right by the gated fenceline. Park in the pullout.

Hiking directions: Walk past the signed trail gate and take the wide jeep road uphill through the lush forest to a posted junction at 0.2 miles. The right fork follows the Maunawili Ditch Trail (Hike 26). Stay on the Maunawili Demonstration Trail, continuing straight ahead on the main path. At a half mile the trail bends sharply to the right to a trail split and a "no horse access" sign. The right fork passes metal posts to a footpath. Stay to the left as the footpath narrows and follows the edge of the cliffs, overlooking the Koolau Mountains, the Waimanalo Valley and Manana Island. Wind along the edge of the mountain into the shady forest. The path crosses the Aniani Nui Ridge and emerges at a steep road and four-way junction at 1.3 miles. This is a good turnaround spot.

To hike further, cross the road and continue on the signed Maunawili Demonstration Trail.

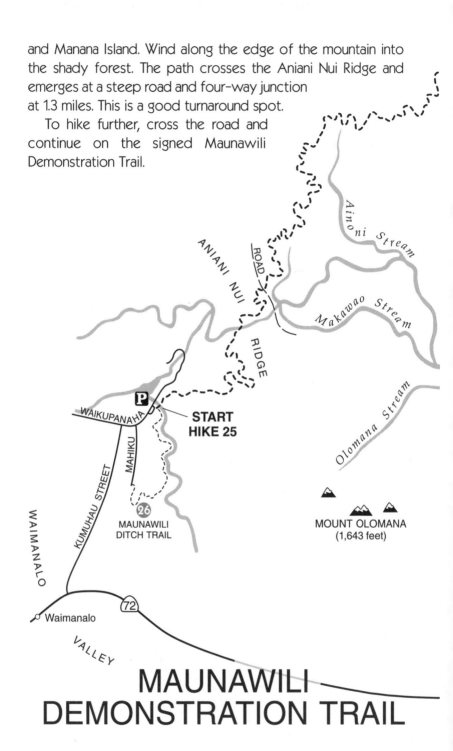

MAUNAWILI DEMONSTRATION TRAIL

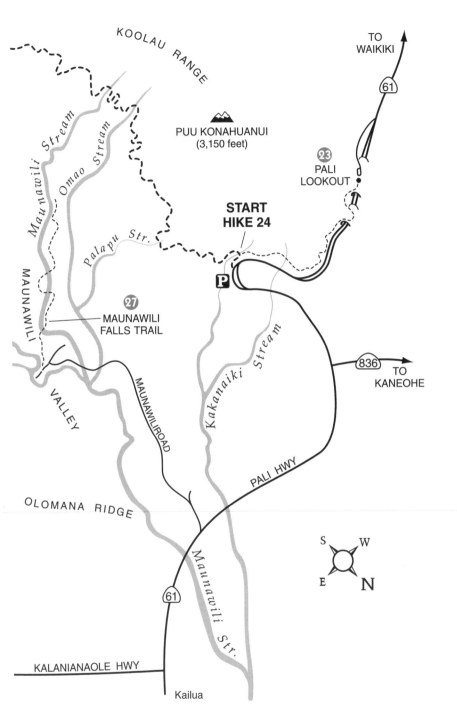

KOOLAU RANGE

Maunawili Stream

Omao Stream

Palapu Str.

PUU KONAHUANUI
(3,150 feet)

TO WAIKIKI

61

23
PALI
LOOKOUT

START
HIKE 24

P

27
MAUNAWILI
FALLS TRAIL

MAUNAWILI

VALLEY

MAUNAWILI ROAD

Kakanaiki Stream

836
TO KANEOHE

OLOMANA RIDGE

PALI HWY

61

Maunawili Str.

KALANIANAOLE HWY

Kailua

S   W

E   N

Hike 26
Maunawili Ditch Trail

Hiking distance: 3 mile loop
Hiking time: 1.5 hours
Elevation gain: 150 feet
Maps: U.S.G.S. Koko Head
      Oahu Reference Maps: Central Oahu/Windward Coast

Summary of hike: The Maunawili Ditch Trail begins on the outskirts of Waimanalo. The loop trail makes an easy meandering hike through a pastoral forest on the lower slopes of the Koolau Range. It is known locally as the "G-Rated Trail" due to its pleasant, gentle grade. The trail shares the first quarter mile with the Maunawili Demonstration Trail—Hike 30. (In reality, the red dirt path follows Kailua Ditch, while the actual Maunawili Ditch is located to the south.)

Driving directions: From Waikiki, take H-1 west 1.5 miles to the Pali Highway (61) north. Drive 9.5 miles north to the end of the Pali Highway in Kailua where the Pali Highway crosses the Kalanianaole Highway (72) and becomes Kailua Road. Turn right on Highway 72, and drive 3.1 miles to Kumuhau Street on the right, just past the Olomana Golf Course. Turn right on Kumuhau Street, and go 1 mile to a T-junction with Waikupanaha Street. Turn right and continue 0.2 miles to the signed trailhead on the right by the gated fenceline. Park in the pullout.

Hiking directions: Walk through the signed trail gate, and follow the wide jeep road uphill through a beautiful forest abundant with birds. At a quarter mile is a signed junction. The left (main) fork continues on the Maunawili Demonstration Trail (Hike 25). Take the Maunawili Ditch Trail to the right on the wide red dirt footpath. The near-level trail winds through the shady forest, curving around the folds of the mountain. At 0.7 miles the path skirts along the back boundary of a tropical fruit nursery. The views extend from the inland mountains to the sloping valley and ocean. At two miles, begin a gradual descent to the other trailhead gate at the end of Mahiku Place. Bear to the right and walk along the road 0.7 miles to Waikupanaha Street. Again bear right, completing the loop at the trailhead pullout.

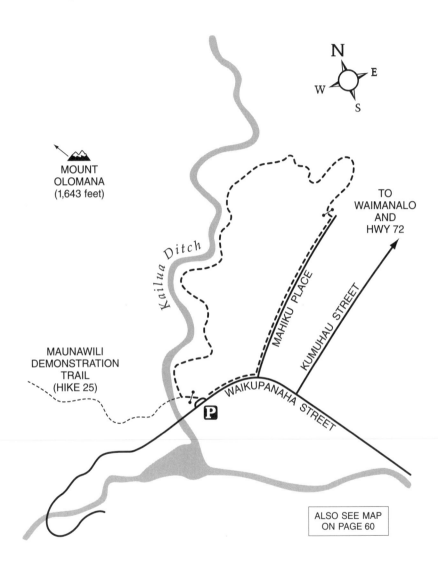

MAUNAWILI
DITCH TRAIL

Hike 27
Maunawili Falls

Hiking distance: 2.6 miles round trip
Hiking time: 1:45 hours
Elevation gain: 400 feet
Maps: U.S.G.S. Koko Head and Honolulu
        Oahu Reference Maps: Central Oahu/Windward Coast

Summary of hike: Maunawili Falls is an alluring 20-foot cataract that cascades off rocky cliffs into a deep pool. The trail to Maunawili Falls is set in a beautiful forest on the slopes of the Koolau Mountains near the town of Maunawili. The path follows Maunawili Stream, and the cascading sounds of the stream are constant throughout the hike. The forested area is rich with banana, papaya, ginger, ti and taro plants.

Driving directions: From Waikiki, take H-1 west to the Pali Highway (61) north. Drive 9 miles to the second Auloa Road turnoff—turn right. At 0.1 mile the road forks. Take the left fork—Maunawili Road. Continue 1.5 miles to the trailhead on the left. Park alongside the curb on Kelewina Street on the right.

Hiking directions: The posted trailhead begins by following an asphalt road about 100 yards to a footpath on the right. Take this footpath, which parallels and crosses Maunawili Stream using rocks as stepping stones. At 0.7 miles, a little over half way, is the third crossing of the stream. From here it is a short climb to a signed junction on a ridge with views of the surrounding Koolau Mountains. Take the left fork and descend to the stream. Boulder hop upstream a short distance to the falls and swimming pool. Return along the same trail.

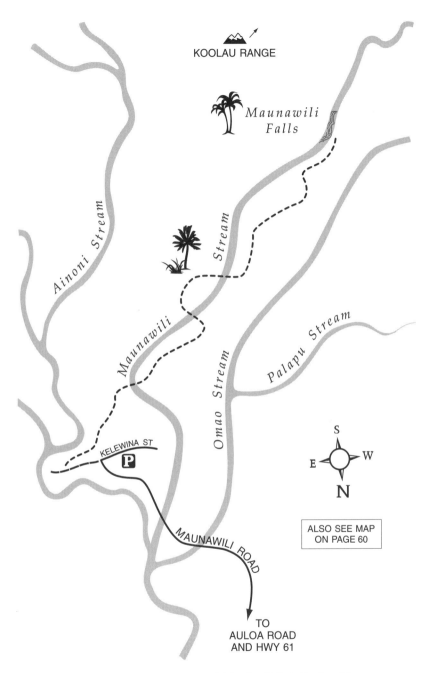

KOOLAU RANGE

Maunawili Falls

Ainoni Stream

Maunawili Stream

Stream

Palapu Stream

Omao Stream

KELEWINA ST
P

S
E ⊕ W
N

ALSO SEE MAP
ON PAGE 60

MAUNAWILI ROAD

TO
AULOA ROAD
AND HWY 61

MAUNAWILI FALLS

Hike 28
Hoomaluhia Botanical Garden

45-680 Luluku Road, Kaneohe
Open daily · 9 a.m.— 4 p.m.

Hiking distance: 1—2 miles
Hiking time: 1 hour (plus browsing time)
Elevation gain: Near level
Maps: U.S.G.S. Kaneeohe
Botanical Garden Map (available at visitor center)

Summary of hike: Hoomaluhia Botanical Garden is situated on 400 sloping acres of former farmland in windward Oahu above Kaneohe. The rainforest garden sits at the foot of the Koolau Mountains beneath the towering Pali Cliffs. An ocean view spreads out to the northeast. The verdant garden serves as a nature conservancy, yet looks more like a natural forest reserve. There are hundreds of flowers, fruits, bushes, vines and trees from tropical regions all over the world. The gardens include a 32-acre manmade lake, streams, footbridges, meadows, a visitor center, picnic pavilions and a network of meandering trails along the lush Koolau foothills.

Driving directions: From Waikiki, take H-1 west 1.5 miles to the Pali Highway (61) north. Drive 7.7 miles north to the junction with the Kamehameha Highway (83) and turn left. Continue 2 miles and turn left on Luluku Road. Drive 1.6 miles to the parking lot and visitor center inside the botanical garden.

Hiking directions: From the visitor center, take the walking path past a few small buildings. The trail continues along the south side of Loko Waimaluhia, a 32-acre reservoir and dam. Paths follow along streams, over footbridges, and in and around the gardens. Explore on your own, choosing your own route and turnaround spot.

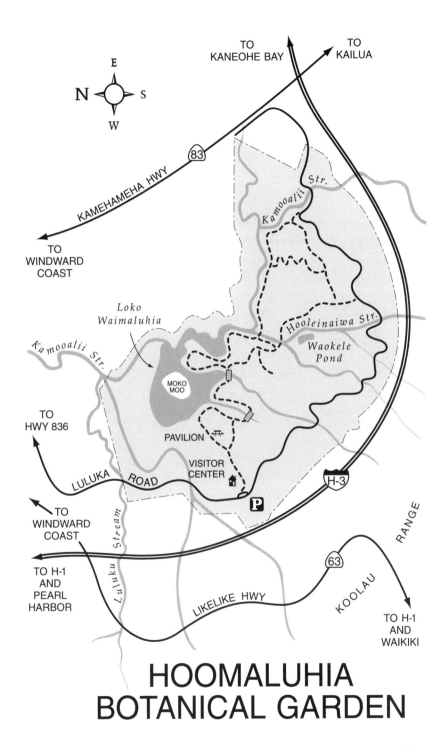

HOOMALUHIA
BOTANICAL GARDEN

Hike 29
Kailua Bay
Oneawa Beach • Kailua Beach • Kailua Beach Park

Hiking distance: 3 miles round trip
Hiking time: 2 hours
Elevation gain: Level
Maps: U.S.G.S. Mokapu
Oahu Reference Maps: Central Oahu/Windward Coast

Summary of hike: This hike is a beach stroll along Kailua Bay beginning at Kailua Beach Park near the pavilion and picnic area. Kailua Bay rests against a two-mile strip of white sand bordered by rocky points. The bay lies between Mokapu Peninsula to the north and Waimanalo Bay to the south. The bay includes Oneawa Beach, Kailua Beach and Kailua Beach Park, a 30-acre park with a large lawn area, shade trees and a wide sand beach. Kaelepulu Canal flows through the pond, dividing the beach park. Just offshore is the seabird sanctuary of Popoia "Flat" Island.

Driving directions: From Waikiki, take H-1 west 1.5 miles to the Pali Highway (61) north. Drive 9.5 miles north to the end of the Pali Highway in Kailua, where the Pali Highway crosses the Kalanianaole Highway (72) and becomes Kailua Road. Continue straight ahead on Kailua Road, into the town of Kailua, to a road split at 1.2 miles. Stay to the left onto Kuulei Road 0.7 miles to Kalaheo Avenue. Turn right and continue 0.4 miles to Kailua Road. Turn left and enter Kailua Beach Park, one block ahead. Park in the lot.

Hiking directions: From the parking lot, walk east towards the ocean past the tree groves and picnic area. At the water's edge, go left, following the shoreline. Mokapu Point and Ulupau Crater in the north are prominent throughout the walk. Stroll along the beach to Kawainui Canal at the north end of the bay or choose your own turnaround spot.

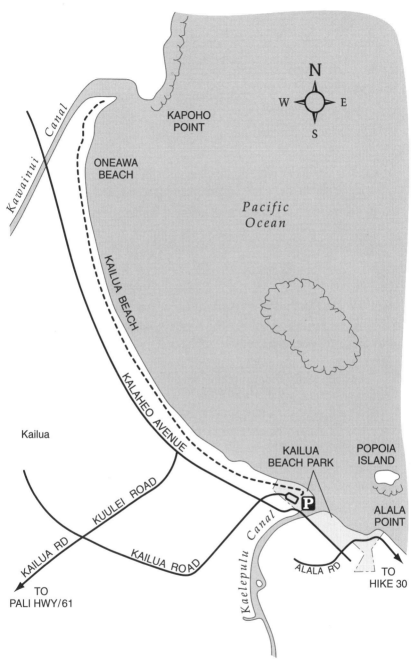

KAILUA BAY

Hike 30
Kaiwa Ridge Trail

Hiking distance: 1.3 miles round trip
Hiking time: 45 minutes
Elevation gain: 500 feet
Maps: U.S.G.S. Mokapu
      Oahu Reference Maps: Central Oahu/Windward Coast

Summary of hike: The Kaiwa Ridge Trail follows the ridge in the Keolu Hills between Kailua Bay and Waimanalo Bay. The trail leads to an ocean lookout at an old military bunker above Lanikai Beach with incredible 360-degree views. The expansive views extend north to Mokapu Peninsula and inland across the Koolau Range. Offshore are the twin Mokulua Islands and Popoia "Flat" Island, all three seabird sanctuaries. The well-defined path is not a designated or maintained trail but is frequently used. The short hike requires some careful footing due to the loose rocks and steepness.

Driving directions: From Waikiki, take H-1 west 1.5 miles to the Pali Highway (61) north. Drive 9.5 miles north to the end of the Pali Highway in Kailua, where the Pali Highway crosses the Kalanianaole Highway (72) and becomes Kailua Road. Continue straight ahead on Kailua Road, which curves right at 1.2 miles and jogs left at 1.7 miles. Reach Kalaheo Avenue at 2.2 miles near the waterfront. Turn right and go 0.5 miles, crossing the bridge over the canal to Alala Road. Turn left 0.3 miles to a road fork. Curve right onto Aalapapa, and drive 0.2 miles to Kaelepulu Drive. Turn right and park in the pullouts on the right adjacent to the Mid Pacific Country Club, or park in the country club parking lot.

Hiking directions: Walk up the private driveway at 275 Kaelepulu Drive. As the driveway curves left, take the footpath to the right alongside the chain-link fence. Climb steeply at first, then level off on a flat landing at an overlook of the windward coast and Mokulua Islands. Follow the eroded ridge to a series of additional flat landings with higher and better views.

Continue on the edge of the cliffs, reaching the graffiti-covered shelter at the summit. The coastal views across Kailua and Waimanalo are superb.

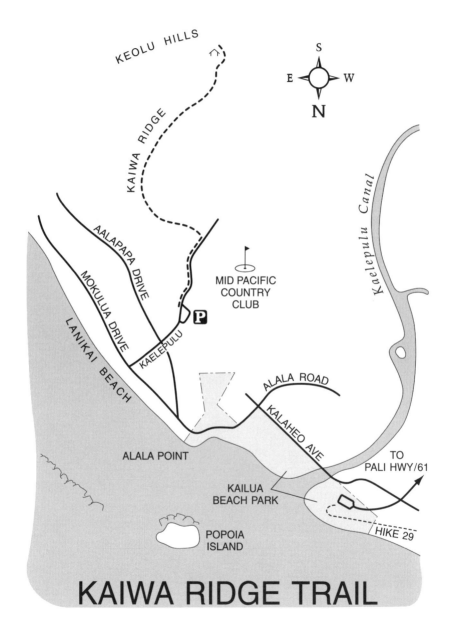

KAIWA RIDGE TRAIL

Hike 31
Waimanalo Bay State Recreation Area

Hiking distance: 1 mile round trip
Hiking time: 30 minutes
Elevation gain: Level
Maps: U.S.G.S. Koko Head
Oahu Reference Maps: Central Oahu/Windward Coast

Summary of hike: Waimanalo Bay is a wide crescent-shaped bay with a 3.5-mile sandy beach. Waimanalo Bay State Recreation Area, known as Sherwood Forest, is a rolling parkland with a heavily wooded ironwood forest backed by the steep Koolau Range. The recreation area is bordered by Puha Stream and Bellows Air Force Base on the north and Aloiloi Street to the south. Off shore are the seabird sanctuaries of Manana and Kaohikaipu Islands.

Driving directions: From McCully Street and King Street in Waikiki, go east on King Street one mile. Curve left and enter H-1 east. Continue 17 miles to the signed park entrance. (Along the way, H-1 becomes the Lunalilo Freeway, which becomes the Kalanianaole Highway/72.) The recreation area is located 8.3 miles beyond the Hanauma Bay turnoff and a quarter mile past McDonald's in the town of Waimanalo. Turn right on the paved road at the opening in the chain-link fence. Follow the park road 0.3 miles to the parking lot.

Hiking directions: Cross the shady rolling parkland towards the ocean. To the left, walk through the forest or follow the shoreline to the north border of the state park at the signed Bellows Air Force Base boundary. Return to the right and head south towards Waimanalo Beach. The state park ends at Aloiloi Street, but you can continue south along Waimanalo Beach. The beach is backed by ironwood trees that act as a barrier between the residential neighborhood. Choose your own turn-around spot.

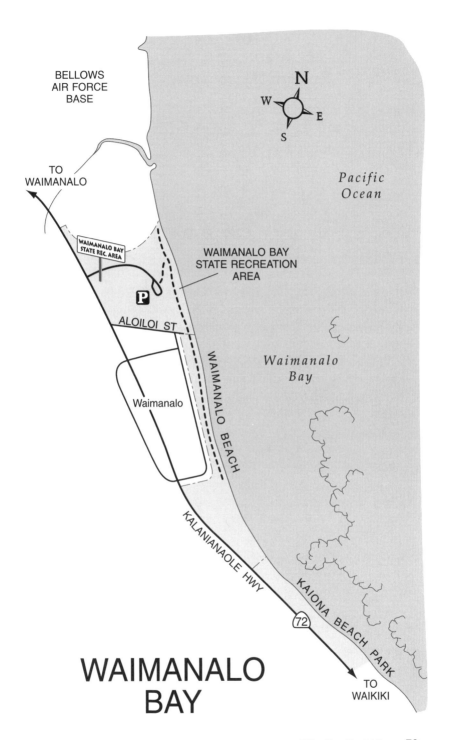

BELLOWS
AIR FORCE
BASE

TO
WAIMANALO

*Pacific
Ocean*

WAIMANALO BAY
STATE REC. AREA

WAIMANALO BAY
STATE RECREATION
AREA

P

ALOILOI ST

*Waimanalo
Bay*

WAIMANALO BEACH

Waimanalo

KALANIANAOLE HWY

KAIONA BEACH PARK

72

WAIMANALO
BAY

TO
WAIKIKI

Hike 32
Aiea Loop Trail
Keaiwa Heiau State Park

Hiking distance: 5 miles round trip
Hiking time: 3 hours
Elevation gain: 1,000 feet
Maps: U.S.G.S. Waipahu and Kaneohe

Summary of hike: Keaiwa Heiau State Park is the site of an ancient healing temple. The park sits in the foothills of the Koolau Range above the town of Aiea. The Aiea Loop Trail snakes along a ridge descending from the Koolau Mountains in the state park. The trail winds through tall forests of eucalyptus, Norfolk Island, koa, ohia, ironwood and guava trees. The well-maintained path passes numerous majestic canyons and has great views of Pearl Harbor, the Koolau Range and Central Oahu.

Driving directions: From Waikiki, take H-1 west to Highway 78 and Aiea. (Stay in the left lanes for the Highway 78 junction.) From Highway 78, take the Aiea exit onto Moanalua Road. From Moanalua Road, turn right on Aiea Heights Drive. Aiea Heights Drive winds its way into Keaiwa Heiau State Park. Drive on this one-way road to its highest point, and park in the parking lot by the trailhead.

Hiking directions: Pick up the trail at the back of the parking lot by the water tank. Hike through the eucalyptus grove with a magnificent root system woven across the red dirt path. Shortly beyond the grove is a level, exposed viewing area of Honolulu. The trail follows the ridge with alternating views of the city on the right and the seemingly endless Koolau Range on the left. Disregard the numerous side paths that descend from the ridge. Continue east to Puu Uau, the highest and easternmost point of the trail. As you pass the far end of the loop, watch the gully for wreckage of a C47 cargo plane from a 1943 crash. Gradually descend to the Aiea Stream. As you near the end of the hike, switchbacks lead out of the gulch to the ridge. Enter a camping area, and climb steps to a parking lot and spur road. Follow the spur road to the main park road, and bear to the right, returning to the trailhead.

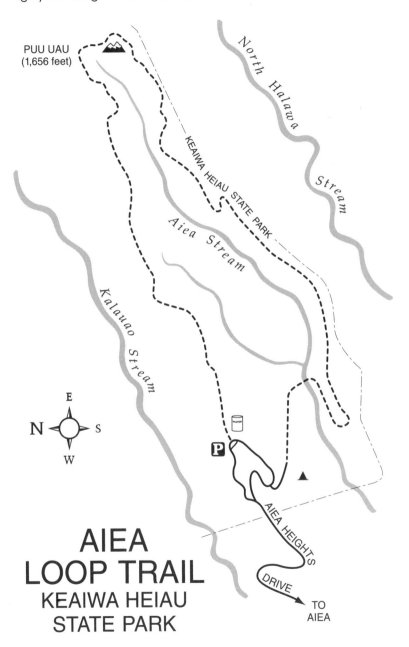

PUU UAU
(1,656 feet)

North Halawa Stream

KEAIWA HEIAU STATE PARK

Aiea Stream

Kalauao Stream

E
N S
W

WATER

P

AIEA HEIGHTS DRIVE

TO AIEA

AIEA LOOP TRAIL
KEAIWA HEIAU STATE PARK

Hike 33
Upper and Lower Waimano Loop Trail

Hiking distance: 2 mile loop
Hiking time: 1 hour
Elevation gain: 300 feet
Maps: U.S.G.S. Waipahu
       Oahu Reference Maps: Central Oahu/Windward Coast

Summary of hike: This pleasant trail makes a loop through the forested Waimano Valley. The upper trail traverses the hillside above the valley, following an abandoned irrigation ditch through groves of guava and mahogany trees with an understory of ferns. The return route on the lower trail parallels Waimano Stream along the valley floor.

Driving directions: From Waikiki, take H-1 west 11 miles to Exit 10/Pearl City. The exit curves to the right onto Moanalua Road, heading northwest. Drive one mile to the road's end. Turn right and continue 1.7 miles on Waimano Home Road to the signed trailhead parking area on the left. The trailhead is located by the security gate at Waimano Home.

Hiking directions: Take the well-marked trail on the left side of the road and chain-link fence. Follow the fenceline 50 yards to the first junction with the Lower Waimano Trail on the left. Begin the loop to the right, staying on the upper trail. At 0.4 miles, leave the fenceline and enter the beautiful, dense forest. Climb a short, steep hill to an overlook of Waimano Canyon, Pearl City, the ocean and, at the west end of the island, the Waianae Range. Descend the north-facing cliffs parallel to an irrigation ditch on the right. Traverse the canyon wall to a signed Y-junction at one mile. The Upper Waimano Trail (Hike 34) continues to the right. Bear left on the Lower Waimano Trail, making a zigzag descent to the streambed. Return downstream through hau groves along the level canyon floor, paralleling Waimano Stream. Gradually angle up the hillside back to the ridge, completing the loop. Return to the trailhead on the right.

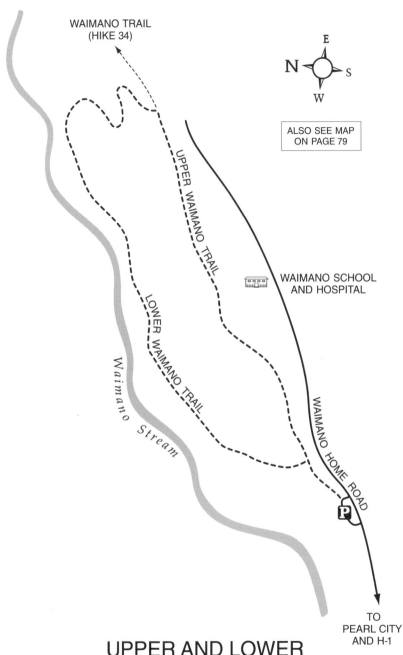

WAIMANO TRAIL
(HIKE 34)

ALSO SEE MAP
ON PAGE 79

UPPER WAIMANO TRAIL

LOWER WAIMANO TRAIL

Waimano Stream

WAIMANO SCHOOL
AND HOSPITAL

WAIMANO HOME ROAD

P

TO
PEARL CITY
AND H-1

UPPER AND LOWER
WAIMANO LOOP TRAIL

Hike 34
Waimano Trail

Hiking distance: 4.5 miles round trip
Hiking time: 2.5 hours
Elevation gain: 300 feet
Maps: U.S.G.S. Waipahu
       Oahu Reference Maps: Central Oahu/Windward Coast

Summary of hike: The Waimano Trail is a forested seven-mile trail that climbs 1,600 feet to a perch high atop the Koolau Mountains. This shorter hike takes in the first couple of miles, heading deeply into the mountains above Waimano Valley. The cliffside trail leads to an overlook of the valley on a ridge with a picnic shelter in a eucalyptus grove.

Driving directions: Follow the driving directions for Hike 33.

Hiking directions: Take the signed path on the left side of the road, following the fenceline to the first junction with the Lower Waimano Trail (Hike 33). Stay on the upper trail along the fenceline. The path leaves the fenceline and enters the lush shady forest at 0.4 miles. Climb a short, steep hill to an overlook of Waimano Canyon, Pearl City, the ocean and the Waianae Range. Descend the north-facing cliffs parallel to a water ditch on the right. Traverse the canyon wall to the second junction with the Lower Waimano Trail on the left at one mile. Stay to the right, crossing small sections of the rock-wall ditch through the deep jungle. The trail narrows on a steep cliff. Careful footing is required, with little room for error. At two miles cross a seasonal stream at the ruins of an old diversion dam. Curve to the right and ascend the hillside on the north canyon wall, curving left towards the ridge. Just below the ridge, a switchback on the left leads to a Boy Scout picnic shelter and overlook. This is our turnaround spot.

To hike further, the main trail follows the ridge, descending to another dam and pool at 3 miles, then steadily climbs to the crest of the Koolau Range at 7 miles.

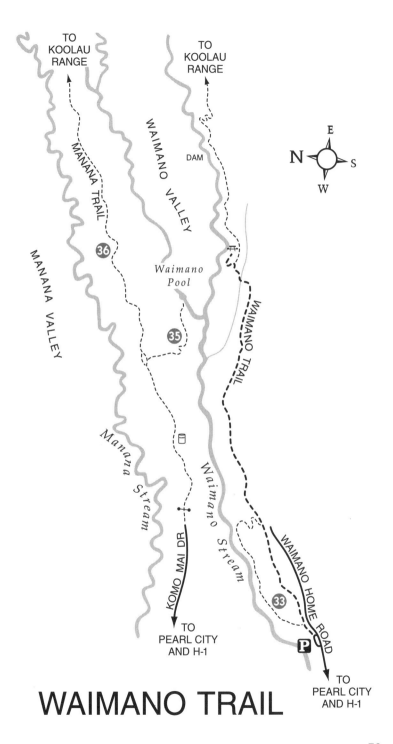

TO
KOOLAU
RANGE

TO
KOOLAU
RANGE

E
N   S
W

MANANA TRAIL

WAIMANO VALLEY

DAM

36

MANANA VALLEY

Waimano Pool

35

WAIMANO TRAIL

Manana Stream

Waimano Stream

KOMO MAI DR

WAIMANO HOME ROAD

33

P

TO
PEARL CITY
AND H-1

TO
PEARL CITY
AND H-1

WAIMANO TRAIL

Hike 35
Manana Trail to Waimano Pool

Hiking distance: 3 miles round trip
Hiking time: 1.5 hours
Elevation gain: 600 feet
Maps: U.S.G.S. Waipahu
       Oahu Reference Maps: Central Oahu/Windward Coast

Summary of hike: Waimano Pool is a swimming hole with a small waterfall deep in the forest in the lush Waimano Valley. The hike follows the first mile of the Manana Trail (Hike 36) atop the ridge that overlooks Manana Valley and Waimano Valley. A steep side path descends into the Waimano Valley to the stream and pool on the valley floor.

Driving directions: From Waikiki, take H-1 west 11 miles to Exit 10/Pearl City. The exit curves to the right onto Moanalua Road, heading northwest. Drive one mile to the road's end. Turn right and continue 0.6 miles on Waimano Home Road to the second stop light at Komo Mai Drive. Turn left and go 3.1 miles to the end of the road.

Hiking directions: Take the signed trailhead at the end of the road. Pass the trail gate on the paved path into the forest. The paved road ends at a water tank on the right at 0.4 miles. Continue northeast along the ridge on the footpath, crossing under two sets of power lines. Various hunter trails veer off the ridge into Manana Valley on the left and Waimano Valley on the right. Stay on the ridge, overlooking both stream-fed jungle canyons. Descend to the base of a large knoll and an unsigned trail fork at one mile. The Manana Trail (Hike 36) curves around the right side of the knoll, returning to the ridge. The path to the pool stays to the right on a distinct trail along the side ridge. Begin the steep descent into Waimano Valley. This steep trail is known locally as "Heart Attack Hill." A rope tied to trailside trees is available for better grip on the steep sections. As you descend, curve left, staying on the main trail. Avoid the temptation of bearing to the right, directly toward the stream. At Waimano Stream, take the left fork a short distance upstream to Waimano Pool and a small waterfall.

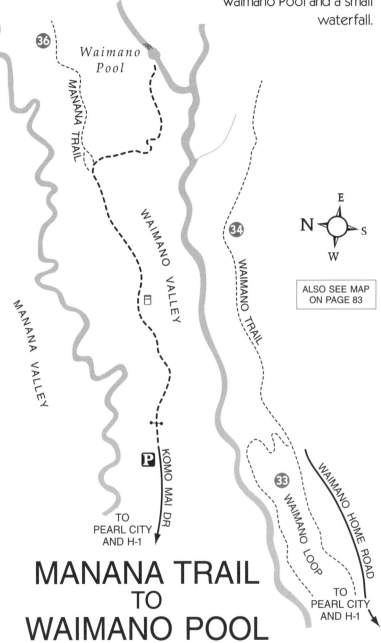

MANANA TRAIL
TO
WAIMANO POOL

Hike 36
Manana Trail

Hiking distance: 4 miles round trip
Hiking time: 2 hours
Elevation gain: 600 feet
Maps: U.S.G.S. Waipahu
Oahu Reference Maps: Central Oahu/Windward Coast

Summary of hike: The Manana Trail follows the ridge between Manana Valley and Waimano Valley through the rainforest for six miles to the summit of the Koolau Range. The trail is a remote, usually muddy, eroded ridge route. This hike takes in the first two miles of the trail over continuous saddles and humps to various overlooks. The trail passes through pristine groves of eucalyptus, guava, koa and a lush undergrowth of low shrubs, moss and ferns.

Driving directions: From Waikiki, take H-1 west 11 miles to Exit 10/Pearl City. The exit curves to the right onto Moanalua Road, heading northwest. Drive one mile to the road's end. Turn right and continue 0.6 miles on Waimano Home Road to the second stop light at Komo Mai Drive. Turn left and go 3.1 miles to the end of the road.

Hiking directions: Take the signed trail past the gate at the end of the road. Follow the paved path into the forest to a water tank on the right at 0.4 miles. Continue along the ridge on the footpath, crossing under two sets of power lines. Various hunter trails veer off the ridge into Manana Valley on the left and Waimano Valley on the right. Stay on the ridge, overlooking the forested stream-fed canyons. At one mile the path descends to the base of a large knoll and an unsigned trail fork. The side path on the right leads into Waimano Valley and Waimano Pool (Hike 35). The Manana Trail curves around both sides of the knoll, returning to the ridge. A shorter but steeper trail heads straight up and over the knoll. A mosaic of exposed roots are intertwined along the muddy path. Contour up and

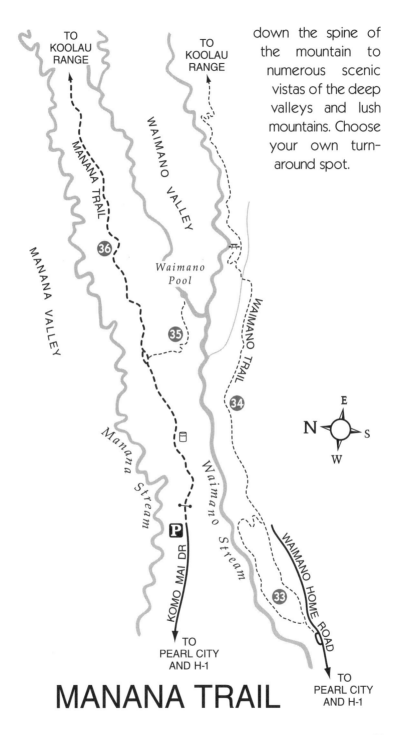

down the spine of the mountain to numerous scenic vistas of the deep valleys and lush mountains. Choose your own turn-around spot.

TO
KOOLAU
RANGE

TO
KOOLAU
RANGE

WAIMANO VALLEY

MANANA TRAIL

MANANA VALLEY

36

Waimano Pool

35

WAIMANO TRAIL

34

Manana Stream

Waimano Stream

N E
S
W

33

WAIMANO HOME ROAD

KOMO MAI DR

P

TO
PEARL CITY
AND H-1

TO
PEARL CITY
AND H-1

MANANA TRAIL

Hike 37
Wahiawa Botanic Garden

1396 California Avenue, Wahiawa
Open daily · 9 a.m.— 4 p.m.

Hiking distance: 1 mile round trip
Hiking time: 1 hour
Elevation gain: 50 feet
Maps: U.S.G.S. Hauula
Oahu Reference Maps: Central Oahu/Windward Coast
Wahiawa Botanical Garden map

Summary of hike: Wahiawa Botanic Garden in central Oahu is one of the five Honolulu Botanical Gardens. The 27-acre garden dates back to the 1920s when the Hawaii Sugar Planters Association leased the land for experimental tree planting. The garden is tucked into a lush, forested ravine at an elevation of 1,000 feet. The cool yet humid garden includes a tropical rainforest, native trees and exotic trees from Africa, Asia, Australia, China, Japan, New Guinea and the Philippines.

Driving directions: From Waikiki, take H-1 west for 16 miles to Exit 8, the H-2/Wahiawa exit. Drive 8 miles north on H-2 to Highway 80 (Kamehameha Highway) in Wahiawa. Bear right on Highway 80 and go 0.4 miles to the third traffic light at California Avenue. Turn right and continue 0.9 miles to the botanical garden and parking lot on the left.

Hiking directions: Before entering the botanic garden, walk to the west end of the parking lot. A bridge spans the gulch, overlooking the magnificent gardens. Return to the entrance building at the east end of the parking lot, and take the paved path winding down the slope into the densely wooded ravine. At the canyon floor, a labyrinth of footpaths weave through the gardens with flowering trees entangled by vines and rich green ferns. Some of the paths are lined with bamboo railings. With so much to explore, meander at your own pace and choose your own route.

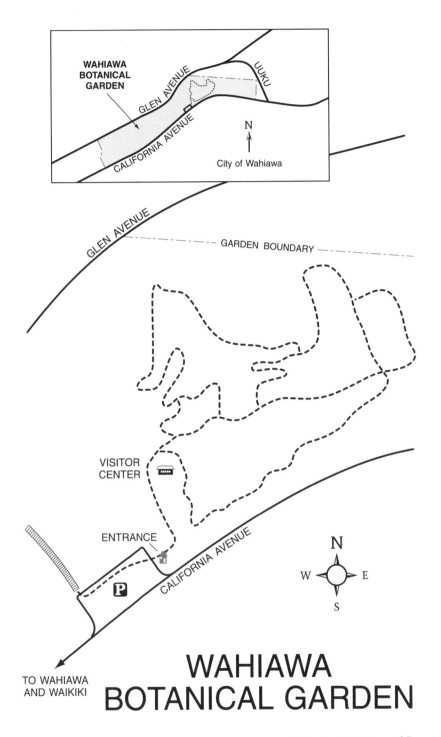

WAHIAWA
BOTANICAL GARDEN

Hike 38
Maili Beach Park

Hiking distance: 3 miles round trip
Hiking time: 1.5 hour
Elevation gain: Level
Maps: U.S.G.S. Waianae
            Oahu Reference Maps: North Shore/Leeward Coast

Summary of hike: Maili Beach Park is a large, palm-lined grassy park with picnic tables and campsites. The park is bordered by two streams and two mountains. At the north end of the park is Mailiilii Stream and picturesque Puu Mailiilii. At the south end is Maili Stream, backed by Puu o Hulu Kai. The park is fronted with a beautiful 1.5-mile strand of white sand with scattered rocks. An exposed marine shelf lines the beach.

Driving directions: From Waikiki, take H-1 west for 25 miles, curving around Pearl Harbor to the leeward coast at Kahe Point. H-1 becomes the Farrington Highway (93) a few miles before reaching the coastline. From Kahe Point, continue 7 miles parallel to the coastline to a quarter-mile long paved parking lot. It is in the town of Maili at the center of Maili Beach Park, across from Liliana Street .

Hiking directions: Cross the expansive lawn and picnic area towards the ocean. Go right (north), following the coastline to the mouth of Mailiilii Stream and a popular swimming area. The stream is bordered by a lava rock jetty and backed by the distinct rounded hill of Puu Mailiilii. Return to the south along the shore, parallel to the exposed coral reef. The beach park ends at the banks of Maili Stream with Puu o Hulu Kai as a backdrop.

To hike further, cross the stream and continue into Maipalaoa Beach, reaching Maili Point in a half mile.

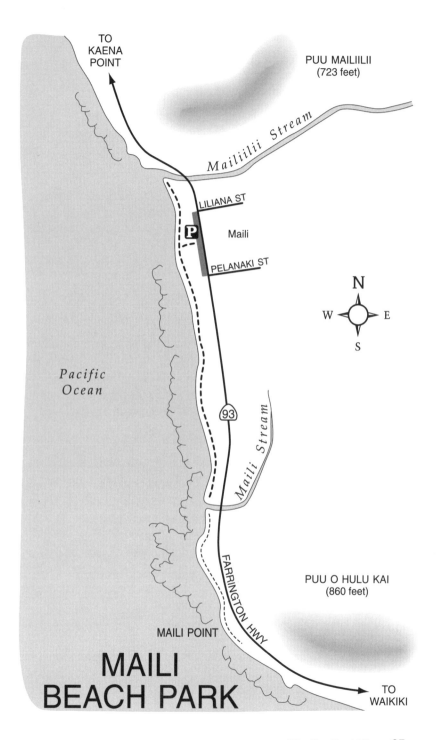

TO
KAENA
POINT

PUU MAILIILII
(723 feet)

Mailiilii Stream

LILIANA ST

P

Maili

PELANAKI ST

N

W   E

S

*Pacific
Ocean*

93

Maili Stream

FARRINGTON HWY

PUU O HULU KAI
(860 feet)

MAILI POINT

TO
WAIKIKI

MAILI
BEACH PARK

Hike 39
Kuilioloa Heiau and Kaneilio Point

Hiking distance: 0.6 miles round trip
Hiking time: 30 minutes
Elevation gain: Level
Maps: U.S.G.S. Waianae
Oahu Reference Maps: North Shore/Leeward Coast

Summary of hike: Kuilioloa Heiau sits on Kaneilio Point, a coconut tree-lined peninsula extending out to sea. The sacred heiau is built on three terraced platforms with sweeping views of the Waianae Coast. The rocky point separates Pokai Bay from Lualualei Beach Park and is backed by the 652-foot Puu Paheehee.

Driving directions: From Waikiki, take H-1 west for 25 miles, curving around Pearl Harbor to the leeward coast at Kahe Point. H-1 becomes the Farrington Highway (93) a few miles before reaching the coastline. From Kahe Point, continue 9 miles parallel to the coastline to Lualualei Homestead Road at a traffic light in Waianae. Turn left and drive one block to the Pokai Bay parking lot straight ahead.

Hiking directions: From the parking lot, walk toward the ocean. Follow the tree-lined path to the grove of coconut palms on Kaneilio Point. The multi-tiered Kuilioloa Heiau is situated on the point overlooking Pokai Bay and Lualualei Beach. With the ocean surrounding the point on three sides, enjoy the panoramic views extending from Lahilahi Point to the north to the Puu o Hulukai and Puu o Uka Mountains to the south. After exploring the heiau and point, return on the path along the south side of the peninsula. There is easy access to the sandy beaches on either side of the peninsula and calm water with a breakwater for swimming in Pokai Bay.

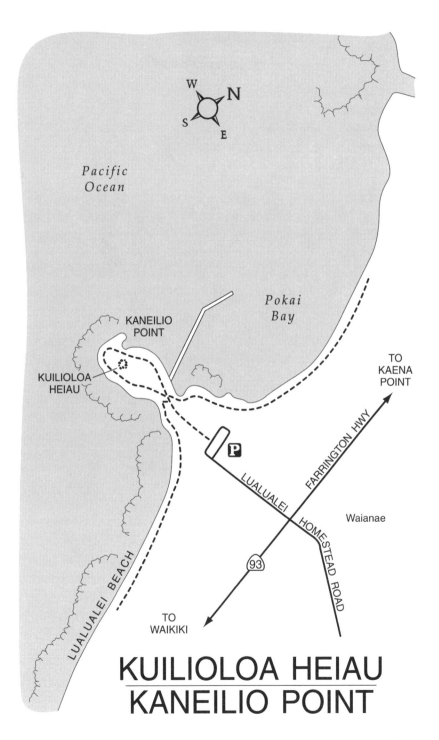

KUILIOLOA HEIAU
KANEILIO POINT

Hike 40
Keaau Beach Park

Hiking distance: 2.5 miles round trip
Hiking time: 1 hours
Elevation gain: Level
Maps: U.S.G.S. Kaena and Waianae
　　　　Oahu Reference Maps: North Shore/Leeward Coast

Summary of hike: Keaau Beach Park is a gorgeous, tree-lined park and picnic ground dotted with palms at the west end of the island. The Waianae Range is the backdrop to this grassy coastal park. To the south, the hike follows the low bluffs parallel to the rocky shoreline and reef to numerous tidepools. To the north, the hike extends to Kalaeopaakai, a black lava point backed by sand dunes

Driving directions: From Waikiki, take H-1 west for 25 miles, curving around Pearl Harbor to the leeward coast at Kahe Point. H-1 becomes the Farrington Highway (93) a few miles before reaching the coastline. From Kahe Point, continue 13.5 miles parallel to the coastline to the signed Keaau Beach parking lot on the left at mile marker 15. The quarter-mile long parking lot borders the highway.

Hiking directions: Walk across the park to the west edge of the grassy flat, reaching the low bluffs lined with lava rock. Bear to the left and head south, following the coastline for a half mile along the grassy picnic area. The path continues onto the coral reef through a maze of tidepools. The park and path end a short distance ahead at a subdivision of homes. Returning to the north, the beach park continues along the bluffs. Less than a mile beyond the Keaau Beach Park boundary is Kalaeopaakai, a lava rock point and sand dunes. Choose your own turnaround spot.

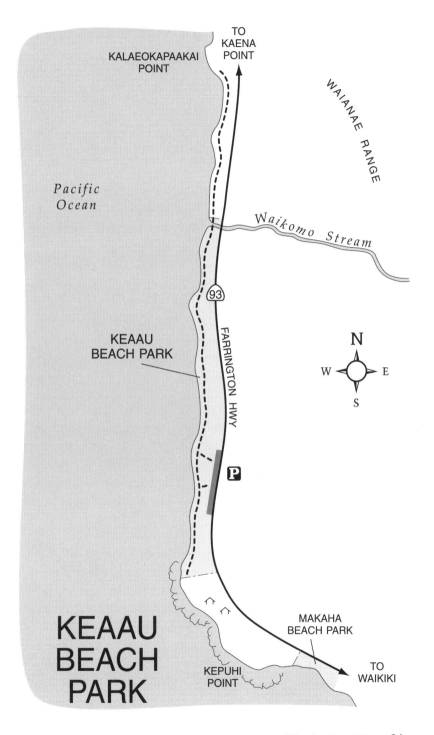

Hike 41
Kaena Point—south access

Hiking distance: 5 miles round trip
Hiking time: 2.5 hours
Elevation gain: Level
Maps: U.S.G.S. Kaena
     Oahu Reference Maps: North Shore/Leeward Coast

map
next page

Summary of hike: Kaena Point is a narrow peninsula at the westernmost tip of Oahu. The Waianae Range tapers to the point, ending at the remote twelve-acre Kaena Point Natural Area Reserve. The exposed reserve is covered with wind-swept dunes, a string of shoreline rocks, sparse vegetation and a beacon. The trail, an old rutted railroad route, parallels the level volcanic coastline, passing tidepools, sea caves, natural arches and blowholes. Kaena Point can be approached from both the south shore and north shore (Hike 42). The two paths merge at the isolated point. This hike begins at the arid south (leeward) shore at the end of the road.

Driving directions: From Waikiki, take H-1 west for 25 miles, curving around Pearl Harbor to the leeward coast at Kahe Point. H-1 becomes the Farrington Highway (93) a few miles before reaching the coastline. From Kahe Point, continue 19 miles paral-lel to the coastline to the end of the paved road at Yokohama Bay Beach. Park in large pullout on the inland side of road.

Hiking directions: Follow the jeep road northwest, sand-wiched between the ocean cliffs and Kuaokala Ridge. The road follows the marine shelf along the scalloped coral and black lava coastline. Fingers of lava stretch out to sea with endless tidepools, overhanging rocks, natural arches and blowholes. Railroad tie remnants from the turn of the century are visible along the path. Cross a small gulch where the road was washed out. Nearing the point, at the west end of the mountain range, is a signed junction. The right fork continues on the old road, curving around the base of the mountains to the north side of

Oahu (Hike 42). Take the left fork into the Kaena Point Natural Area on the exposed rock-lined footpath. Cross the dunes towards the beacon, which can be seen near the point. Beyond the beacon, explore the sandy point, choosing your own route.

Hike 42
Kaena Point—north access

Hiking distance: 5.5 miles round trip
Hiking time: 2.5 hours
Elevation gain: Level
Maps: U.S.G.S. Kaena
       Oahu Reference Maps: North Shore/Leeward Coast

map
next page

Summary of hike: Kaena Point is located at the arid west end of Oahu. The Waianae Range tapers to a point where the north and south shores merge, forming the remote peninsula. At the point, the twelve-acre Kaena Point Natural Area Reserve protrudes across the windswept dunes past a beacon. Huge waves from both shores crash against the lava rocks that band the point. Kaena Point can be approached from either the north or south shore (Hike 41). The two paths merge at the isolated point. This hike begins on the north shore.

Driving directions: From Waikiki, take H-1 west for 16 miles to Exit 8, the H-2/Wahiawa exit. Drive 8 miles north on H-2 to Highway 99 in Wahiawa. Take Highway 99 for 1.5 miles to a road split with Highway 803. Bear left on Highway 803 (Kaukonahua Road) towards Waialua, and go 7 miles to Highway 930, the Farrington Highway. Bear left on Highway 930 and drive 7.5 miles to the end of the paved road. Park in the sandy pullouts on the side of the road.

Hiking directions: Head west on the unpaved road to the trailhead gate past large boulders. Two parallel trails lead to the point—the old rutted road and the serpentine shoreline trail. Both trails parallel the coastline past sea-cut cliffs, deserted beaches and secluded coves. Continue west across the wide open space along the base of Kuaokala Ridge. At 2 miles, large lava boulders block the road at the gate entrance to Keana Point Natural Reserve. Pass through the gate, and continue towards the point to a trail split at the end of the mountain range. The road curves left along the talus slope, following the base of the mountain to the leeward coast. The right fork crosses the dunes towards the beacon, which can be seen near the point. Beyond the beacon, explore the awesome point, choosing your own route.

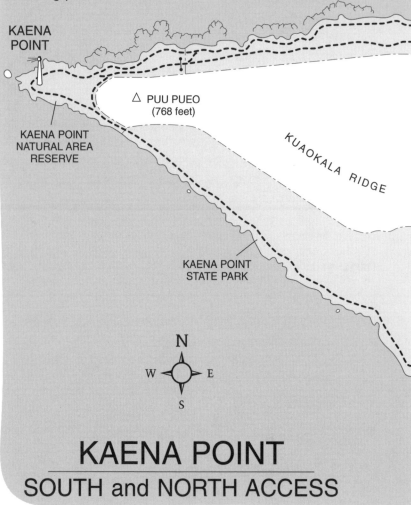

KAENA POINT

KAENA POINT NATURAL AREA RESERVE

△ PUU PUEO
(768 feet)

KUAOKALA RIDGE

KAENA POINT STATE PARK

N
W ← ◇ → E
S

KAENA POINT
SOUTH and NORTH ACCESS

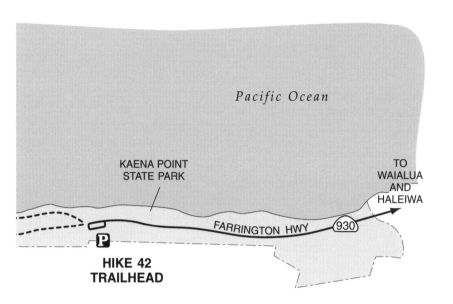

Pacific Ocean

KAENA POINT
STATE PARK

TO
WAIALUA
AND
HALEIWA

FARRINGTON HWY (930)

P

**HIKE 42
TRAILHEAD**

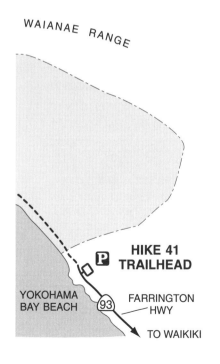

WAIANAE RANGE

P **HIKE 41
TRAILHEAD**

YOKOHAMA
BAY BEACH (93)

FARRINGTON
HWY

TO WAIKIKI

Hike 43
Kaiaka Bay Beach Park

Hiking distance: 2 miles round trip
Hiking time: 1 hour
Elevation gain: Level
Maps: U.S.G.S. Haleiwa
        Oahu Reference Maps: North Shore/Leeward Coast

Summary of hike: Kaiaka Bay Beach Park sits along the Kaiaka Point peninsula near the towns of Waialua and Haleiwa. The grassy beach park is backed by the chiseled Waianae Mountains. Kaiaka Point divides Kaiaka Bay and Waialua Bay. This hike follows the perimeter of the point into both bays.

Driving directions: From Waikiki, take H-1 west for 16 miles to Exit 8, the H-2/Wahiawa exit. Drive 8 miles north on H-2 to Highway 99 in Wahiawa. Take Highway 99/Kamehameha Highway north to the Weed Circle round-about, just south of Haleiwa. Take Highway 82, the Wailua Beach Road, 0.8 miles to Haleiwa Road. Turn right and continue 0.7 miles to the signed Kaiaka Bay Beach Park on the left. Turn left and go a half mile into the park. Park in the spaces along the right side of the road.

Hiking directions: Cross the large grassy area to the ocean-front. Bear left towards Kaiaka Bay parallel to the jagged lava rocks bordering the shoreline. The rocks are backed by hard packed sand and low growing naupaka plants. Follow the edge of the park into the bay. The path ends at the confluence of Paukauila and Kiikii Stream where the wide streams empty into the bay. Returning to the right, follow the shoreline parallel to the sea to a grove of large ironwood trees. From the grove, the path drops into the southern reaches of Waialua Bay. The path follows the bay to Haleiwa Harbor. Choose your own route and distance.

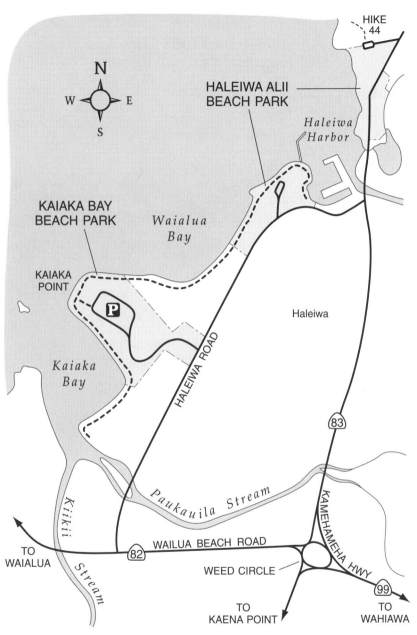

KAIAKA BAY
BEACH PARK

Hike 44
Puaena Point to
Papailoa "Police" Beach

Hiking distance: 2 miles round trip
Hiking time: 1 hour
Elevation gain: Level
Maps: U.S.G.S. Haleiwa
       Oahu Reference Maps: North Shore/Leeward Coast

Summary of hike: This hike begins at the north end of Haleiwa Alii Beach Park and follows the north tip of Waialua Bay past Puaena Point. At the lava rock point are tidepools and sweeping views across Waialua Bay to the Waianae Mountains. Green sea turtles frequent this area. The trail then drops into Papailoa Beach, also known as Police Beach because the Hawaii Police have a lease on the beach for recreational fun.

Driving directions: From Waikiki, take H-1 west for 16 miles to Exit 8, the H-2/Wahiawa exit. Drive 8 miles north on H-2 to Highway 99 in Wahiawa. Take Highway 99/Kamehameha Highway north to the Weed Circle round-about, just south of Haleiwa. Take Highway 83/Kamehameha Highway 1.6 miles, passing through the town of Haleiwa, to Kahalewai Place at the north end of Haleiwa Alii Beach Park. Turn left and park in the lot ahead.

Hiking directions: The trail begins to the right (north) by the gated unpaved road. Pass the gate and walk through the palm tree grove. Begin the loop to the left, leaving the road. The path quickly reaches the oceanfront in an ironwood grove. Bear right, curving around the forest-lined cove past lava formations and tidepools. Cross the formations to Puaena Point jutting into the open sea. After Puaena Point and Waiamua Bay, the trail follows the coastline along the rocky shoreline into Papailoa Beach. To return, curve inland a short distance, and connect with the unpaved service road. Take the road to the right, winding through the forest. Complete the loop near the entrance gate and trailhead.

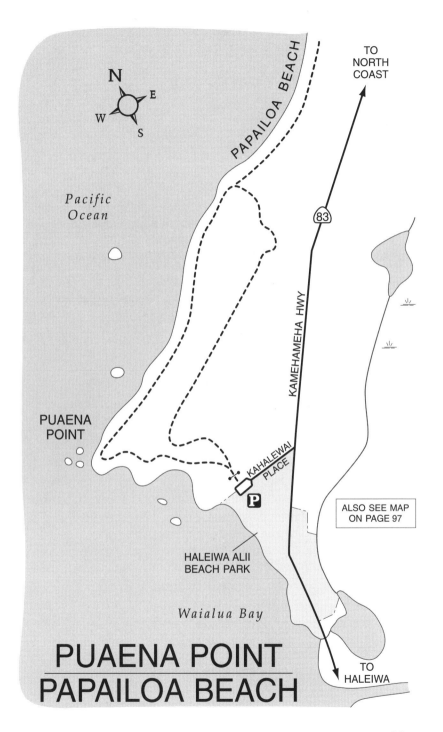

PUAENA POINT
PAPAILOA BEACH

Hike 45
Pupukea Beach Park

Hiking distance: 1.2 miles round trip
Hiking time: 1 hour
Elevation gain: Level
Maps: U.S.G.S. Waimea
   Oahu Reference Maps: North Shore/Leeward Coast

Summary of hike: Pupukea Beach Park, a Marine Life Conservation Area, is a long, narrow park adjacent to Waimea Bay. At the south end of the eighty-acre park is Three Tables, a protected beach with three sections of flat coral reefs. At the north end of the park is a wall of coral reef that forms an enclosed lagoon known as Shark's Cove. The large cove is a snorkeling and beachcombing paradise with tidepools, lava cave formations and blowholes. A walking and biking path lines the back of the beach along an elevated grassy area with groves of ironwoods.

Driving directions: From Waikiki, take H-1 west for 16 miles to Exit 8, the H-2/Wahiawa exit. Drive 8 miles north on H-2 to Highway 99 in Wahiawa. Take Highway 99/Kamehameha Highway north to the Weed Circle round-about, just south of Haleiwa. Take Highway 83, the Kamehameha Highway, a short distance into the town of Haleiwa. From Haleiwa, continue 5 miles northeast on Highway 83 to the signed parking area on the ocean side of the highway, across from Foodland Market at Pupukea Road.

Hiking directions: Head south (left) on the walking path towards Waimea Bay. The path overlooks Three Tables and extends out to the lava rock point adjacent to Waimea Bay. Returning to the north, follow the grassy path along the back end of the beach towards Shark's Cove. At the cove, cross the coral to the enclosed pool. Explore the magnificent area, choosing your own route.

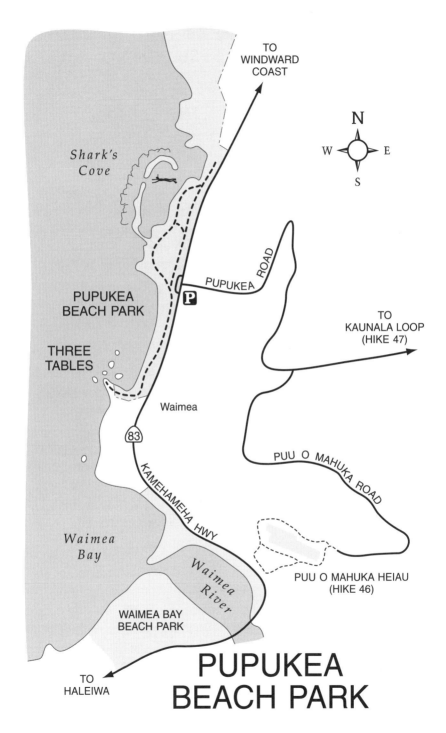

TO
WINDWARD
COAST

N
W E
S

Shark's
Cove

PUPUKEA ROAD

PUPUKEA

P

TO
KAUNALA LOOP
(HIKE 47)

PUPUKEA
BEACH PARK

THREE
TABLES

Waimea

83

PUU O MAHUKA ROAD

KAMEHAMEHA HWY

Waimea
Bay

Waimea
River

PUU O MAHUKA HEIAU
(HIKE 46)

WAIMEA BAY
BEACH PARK

TO
HALEIWA

PUPUKEA
BEACH PARK

Hike 46
Puu O Mahuka Heiau State Monument

Hiking distance: 0.4 mile loop
Hiking time: .5 hour
Elevation gain: Level
Maps: U.S.G.S. Waimea
         Oahu Reference Maps: North Shore/Leeward Coast

Summary of hike: Puu O Mahuka Heiau is the largest and oldest heiau (place of worship) on Oahu. The split-level temple with terraced walls consists of three adjoining stone structures. The temple is poised on the 250-foot cliffs above Waimea Bay, offering sweeping vistas of the scalloped north shore and Waimea Valley. The ancient temple served as a heiau of human sacrifice. Rocks outline a path that circles the 5.7-acre national historic landmark.

Driving directions: From Waikiki, take H-1 west for 16 miles to Exit 8, the H-2/Wahiawa exit. Drive 8 miles north on H-2 to Highway 99 in Wahiawa. Take Highway 99/Kamehameha Highway, north to the Weed Circle round-about, just south of Haleiwa. Take Highway 83, the Kamehameha Highway, a short distance into the town of Haleiwa. From Haleiwa, continue 5 miles northeast on Highway 83 to the Foodland Market on the right at Pupukea Road. Turn right on Pupukea Road and climb the steep road 0.6 miles to Puu O Mahuka Road. Turn right and follow the narrow road 0.7 miles to a parking lot for the Heiau State Monument at the end of the road.

Hiking directions: Bear right on the path, walking counter-clockwise around the perimeter of the rock-walled heiau. A side path leads into the heiau to an alter with fresh religious offerings of leis, fruit and ti leaves wrapped around rocks. Continue around the heiau on the exposed plateau to the edge of the bluffs overlooking Waimea Bay. Panoramic coastal views extend across the bay to the Waianae Range and Kaena Point at the west end of the island.

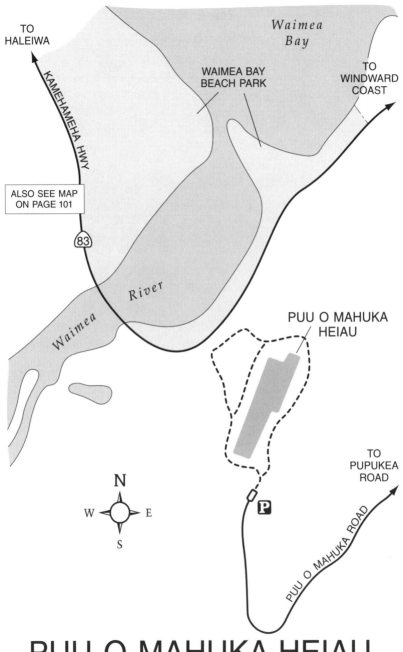

TO
HALEIWA

*Waimea
Bay*

WAIMEA BAY
BEACH PARK

TO
WINDWARD
COAST

KAMEHAMEHA HWY

ALSO SEE MAP
ON PAGE 101

83

River

Waimea

PUU O MAHUKA
HEIAU

TO
PUPUKEA
ROAD

N

W — E

S

P

PUU O MAHUKA ROAD

PUU O MAHUKA HEIAU
STATE MONUMENT

Hike 47
Kaunala Loop

Open to the public on weekends and holidays only.
Do not let the "Private Property—No Trespassing" signs stop you.
Staying on the road to the foot trail is permissible.

Hiking distance: 5 mile loop
Hiking time: 3 hours
Elevation gain: 900 feet
Maps: U.S.G.S. Waimea and Kahuku
Oahu Reference Maps: North Shore/Leeward Coast

Summary of hike: The Kaunala Trail, in the Pupukea Paumalu Forest Reserve, is a favorite hike with a wide cross section of natural features. The diverse hike includes lush tropical forests, jungle stream crossings, forested valleys, ridges and sweeping ridgetop vistas of the mountains and coastline. The serpentine path winds through a forest canopy with groves of eucalyptus, ohia, kukui, ironwood, mahogany, silk and Norfolk Island pine.

Driving directions: From Waikiki, take H-1 west for 16 miles to Exit 8, the H-2/Wahiawa exit. Drive 8 miles north on H-2 to Highway 99 in Wahiawa. Take Highway 99/Kamehameha Highway, north to the Weed Circle round-about, just south of Haleiwa. Take Highway 83, the Kamehameha Highway, a short distance into the town of Haleiwa. From Haleiwa, continue 5 miles northeast on Highway 83 to Foodland Market at Pupukea Road. Turn right on Pupukea Road, and drive until the public road ends at a gate with private property notices. Park off road near the gate.

Hiking directions: Hike to the end of the tree-lined public road to a locked military gate. Go around the gate past the hunter check-in booth. Follow the unpaved road for a half mile to a grove of paperbark trees. Watch for the signed Kaunala Trail on the left. Take the footpath and zigzag down the contours of the hillside to Paumalu Stream. Slowly climb up the hillside on the winding path to a jeep road on the ridge. Bear right and head uphill along the road. Follow the ridge to the high point of the hike—a flat clearing at 1,403 feet with panoramic vistas. Descend from the summit to a gate and cross over it, reaching a junction with the military access road. Go to the right and return on the main trail back to the trailhead.

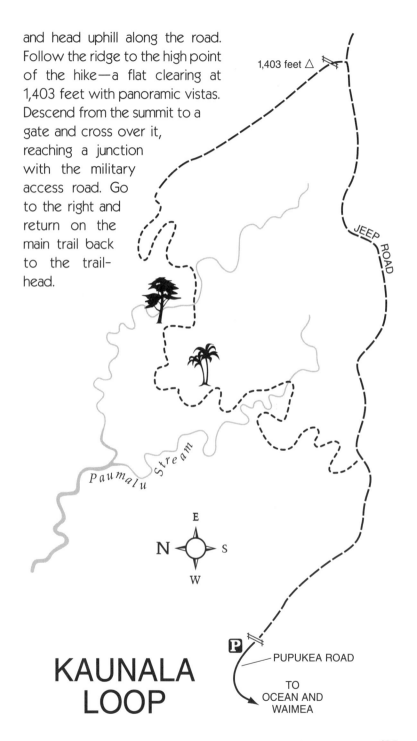

1,403 feet △

JEEP ROAD

Paumalu Stream

E

N ← ◇ → S

W

KAUNALA
LOOP

P

PUPUKEA ROAD

TO
OCEAN AND
WAIMEA

Hike 48
Turtle Bay

Hiking distance: 1.8 miles round trip
Hiking time: 1 hour
Elevation gain: Level
Maps: U.S.G.S. Kahuku
        Oahu Reference Maps: North Shore/Leeward Coast

Summary of hike: Turtle Bay is a long, crescent bay at the northern tip of Oahu. The bay, lined by a tropical ironwood forest, is fronted by rock and coral reefs with small white sand pockets. The bay lies between Kawela Bay and Kuilima Point. This hike follows the Turtle Bay coastline and the perimeter of Kuilima Point into Kuilima Cove. The cove is a small sandy inlet protected by reef, offering safe year-round swimming.

Driving directions: From Waikiki, take H-1 west 3.5 miles to Likelike Highway (63), and head northeast to the windward coast. After crossing the mountains, there are two driving options. The shorter, more direct route is the Kahekili Highway (83)—turn left (north) off the Likelike Highway at 7.5 miles. The more scenic but longer route is the Kamehameha Highway (836), a half mile further on the Likelike Highway (63). Both 83 and 836 merge together about 4.5 miles up the coast. From this junction drive 24.5 miles northwest on Highway 83 to the signed Hilton Turtle Bay Resort turnoff. Turn right on Kuilima Drive, and drive 0.6 miles to the parking lot. A parking fee is required.

From the town of Haleiwa on the north shore, Turtle Bay is 10 miles northeast along Highway 83.

Hiking directions: The Hilton Hotel sits on Kuilima Point and offers the only access spot to the bay. Walk towards the hotel and descend steps on the left side. At the pool, take the foot-path on the left down to the reef on the north end of the bay. A narrow crescent of sand lines the bay, backed by ironwood trees. Continue southwest past a series of reefs and tidepools.

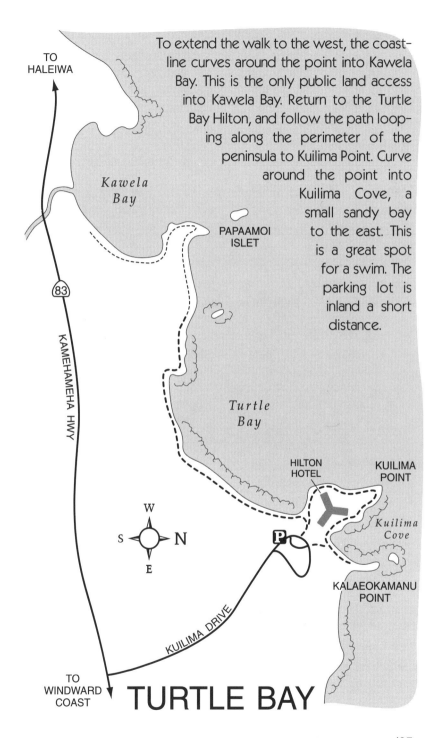

TO
HALEIWA

To extend the walk to the west, the coast-line curves around the point into Kawela Bay. This is the only public land access into Kawela Bay. Return to the Turtle Bay Hilton, and follow the path looping along the perimeter of the peninsula to Kuilima Point. Curve around the point into Kuilima Cove, a small sandy bay to the east. This is a great spot for a swim. The parking lot is inland a short distance.

Kawela Bay

PAPAAMOI
ISLET

83

KAMEHAMEHA HWY

Turtle Bay

HILTON
HOTEL

KUILIMA
POINT

Kuilima Cove

W

S — N

E

P

KALAEOKAMANU
POINT

KUILIMA DRIVE

TO
WINDWARD
COAST

TURTLE BAY

Hike 49
Malaekahana State Recreation Area

Hiking distance: 1.8 miles round trip
Hiking time: 1 hour
Elevation gain: Level
Maps: U.S.G.S. Kahuku
       Oahu Reference Maps: Central Oahu/Windward Coast

Summary of hike: Malaekahana State Recreation Area is a 110-acre wooded beach park that straddles two idyllic bays and is backed by the steep Koolau Range. The hike follows the forested coastline through the tree-shaded park, beginning at one bay then dropping into the other. Mokuaula "Goat" Island, a seabird sanctuary, sits a short distance off the point. In calm weather and at low tide, the island can be reached by foot.

Driving directions: From Waikiki, take H-1 west 3.5 miles to Likelike Highway (63), and head northeast to the windward coast. After crossing the mountains, there are two driving options. The shorter, more direct route is the Kahekili Highway (83)—turn left (north) off the Likelike Highway at 7.5 miles. The more scenic but longer route is the Kamehameha Highway (836), a half mile further on the Likelike Highway (63). Both 83 and 836 merge together about 4.5 miles up the coast. From this junction drive 19.5 miles northwest on Highway 83 to the signed Malaekahana State Recreation Area on the right between mile markers 17 and 18. The park is a half mile past the Polynesian Cultural Center. Turn right and go 0.2 miles to the parking lot.

    From the town of Haleiwa on the north shore, Malaekahana State Recreation Area is 15 miles northeast along Highway 83.

Hiking directions: Walk through the lush, shady ironwood and pandanus groves up a small hill to the coastline. Beyond the park's north border, in Malaekahana Bay, are beachfront homes. Heading east, either follow the wide paths under the forest canopy or beachcomb to Kalanai Point, the closest spot to Goat Island. Continue south through the forest to Hukilau Beach at the Malaekahana State Recreation Area boundary, where the forested parkland makes way to the sandy beach. To hike further, follow the sandy beach past Hukilau Beach and ocean-front homes into Laie Beach.

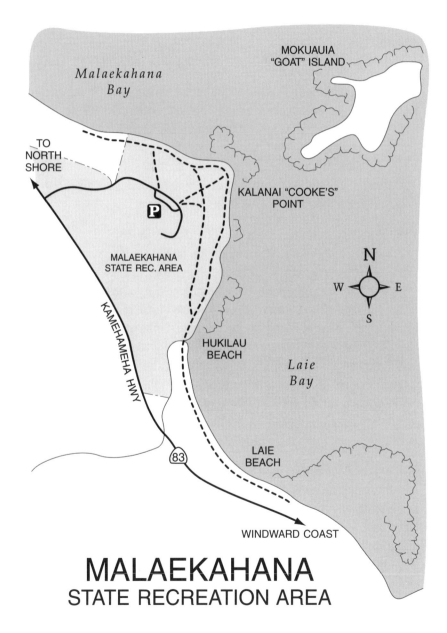

MALAEKAHANA
STATE RECREATION AREA

Hike 50
Kokololio Beach Park

Hiking distance: 1 mile round trip
Hiking time: 30 minutes
Elevation gain: Level
Maps: U.S.G.S. Kahuku
        Oahu Reference Maps: Central Oahu/Windward Coast

Summary of hike: Kokololio Beach is a beautiful forested park fronting a white sand beach. The long, curving shoreline is exposed to the open sea. This hike strolls through the rolling lawns, tree groves and sandy shoreline. The hike can be extended north to the limestone cliffs of Palikilola Point at Bath Tub Beach. To the south the hike continues to the shoreline reefs and tidepools at Kakela Beach.

Driving directions: From Waikiki, take H-1 west 3.5 miles to Likelike Highway (63), and head northeast to the windward coast. After crossing the mountains, there are two driving options. The shorter, more direct route is the Kahekili Highway (83)—turn left (north) off the Likelike Highway at 7.5 miles. The more scenic but longer route is the Kamehameha Highway (836), a half mile further on the Likelike Highway (63). Both 83 and 836 merge together about 4.5 miles up the coast. From this junction drive 16.5 miles northwest to the quarter-mile long parking lot on the right between mile markers 20 and 21.

From the town of Haleiwa on the north shore, the parking lot is 18 miles northeast along Highway 83.

Hiking directions: Head left (north) beyond Kokololio Beach and the beachfront homes at Mahakea Beach. Continue north to the rocky limestone cliffs of Palikilola Point at Bath Tub Beach. Beyond the point, the route leads to Pounders Beach, a long, wide beach popular for bodysurfing. Return to Kokololio Beach and head south. Stroll through the grassy lawn and tree groves of Kokololio Park, or follow the beautiful crescent-shaped beach with reefs and tidepools. Choose your own turnaround spot.

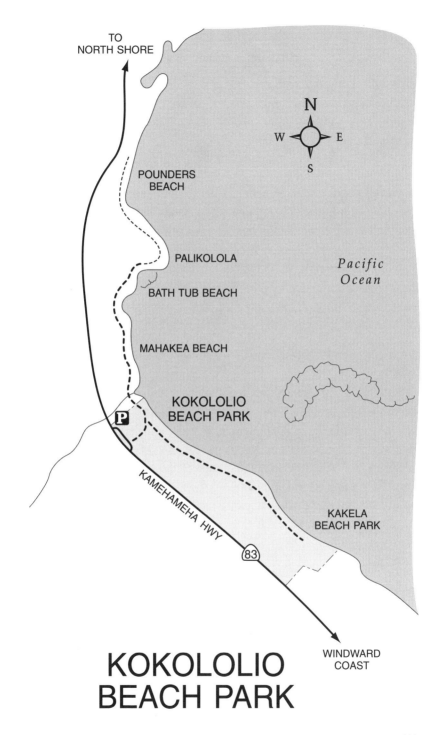

TO
NORTH SHORE

N

W · E

S

POUNDERS
BEACH

PALIKOLOLA

BATH TUB BEACH

*Pacific
Ocean*

MAHAKEA BEACH

**KOKOLOLIO
BEACH PARK**

P

KAMEHAMEHA HWY

83

KAKELA
BEACH PARK

WINDWARD
COAST

KOKOLOLIO
BEACH PARK

Hike 51
Hauula Loop Trail

Hiking distance: 2.5 mile loop
Hiking time: 1.5 hours
Elevation gain: 600 feet
Maps: U.S.G.S. Hauula
        Oahu Reference Maps: Central Oahu/Windward Coast

Summary of hike: The Hauula Loop Trail is a beautiful mountain hike in the Kaipapau Forest Reserve above Hauula. The trail crosses Waipilopilo Gulch and winds up the hillside through an ironwood, Norfolk Island pine and paperback eucalyptus forest with lush fern and moss undergrowth. Fallen needles from the trees carpet the path with a thick matting. From the ridge are panoramic views of Kaipapau Valley, the Koolau Range and the eastern coastline.

Driving directions: From Waikiki, take H-1 west 3.5 miles to Likelike Highway (63), and head northeast to the windward coast. After crossing the mountains, there are two driving options. The shorter, more direct route is the Kahekili Highway (83)—turn left (north) off the Likelike Highway at 7.5 miles. The more scenic but longer route is the Kamehameha Highway (836), a half mile further on the Likelike Highway (63). Both 83 and 836 merge together about 4.5 miles up the coast. From this junction drive 15.5 miles northwest to Kukuna Road, between mile markers 21 and 22 in the town of Hauula. Turn left and take Kukuna Road to the stop sign. Turn right on Hauula Homestead Road 0.2 miles to Maakua Road. Turn left and park at the end of the street by the trail sign.

From the town of Haleiwa on the north shore, Kukuna Road is 19 miles northeast along Highway 83.

Hiking directions: Walk inland on the spur road to the trail sign. Cross the dry streambed to a trail junction about 70 yards ahead. The Maakua Gulch Trail and Papali-Maakua Ridge Trail (Hike 52) bear left. Take the right fork across the gulch, and gently climb up several switchbacks to a trail split. Begin the loop to the left, climbing up the hillside through dense, shady thickets to the ridge overlooking the canyons, mountains and ocean. Descend into Waipilopilo Gulch, and cross the ravine to the next ridge overlooking Kaipapau Valley. Curve to the right, returning on the crest of the narrow ridge towards the ocean. Recross Waipilopilo Gulch and descend on switchbacks, completing the loop. Retrace your steps to the left.

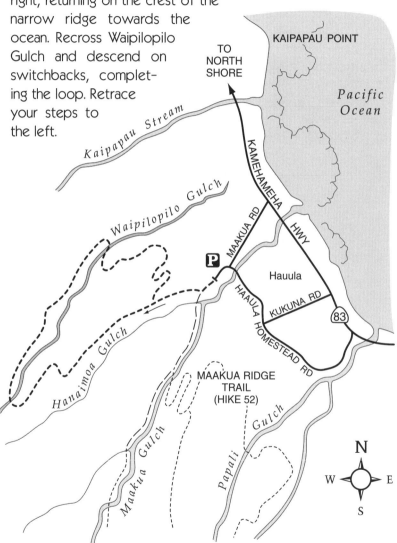

HAUULA LOOP TRAIL

Hike 52
Maakua Ridge Trail and Papali Gulch

Hiking distance: 3 mile loop
Hiking time: 1.5 hours
Elevation gain: 800 feet
Maps: U.S.G.S. Hauula
      Oahu Reference Maps: Central Oahu/Windward Coast

Summary of hike: The Maakua Ridge Trail sits above the town of Hauula in the Kaipapau Forest Reserve. The trail begins in Maakua Gulch and crosses over Maakua Ridge into Papali Gulch, forming a loop. The forested path winds through lush groves of hau, Norfolk Island pines, hala, acacia and kukui trees with a lush understory of ferns and mosses. From the ridge are vistas of the Koolau Range, Maakua Gulch, the surrounding countryside and the windward coast.

Driving directions: Follow the driving directions for Hike 51.

Hiking directions: Walk inland on the spur road to the trail sign. Cross the dry streambed to a junction about 70 yards ahead. The Hauula Trail (Hike 51) bears right. Stay in Maakua Gulch on the old road to the left about 200 yards to a posted junction. Bear left on the Maakua Ridge Trail, crossing Maakua Gulch. Switchbacks lead up the hillside to a trail split. Begin the loop to the right, climbing to the ridgeline. Descend into Papali Gulch and cross the stream. Curve left, gradually ascending the hillside to the next ridge. Return to the north and traverse the shady slopes above Punaiki Gulch. Zigzag down the hill and recross Papali Gulch. Curve inland, climbing out of the gulch and completing the loop. Retrace your steps to the right.

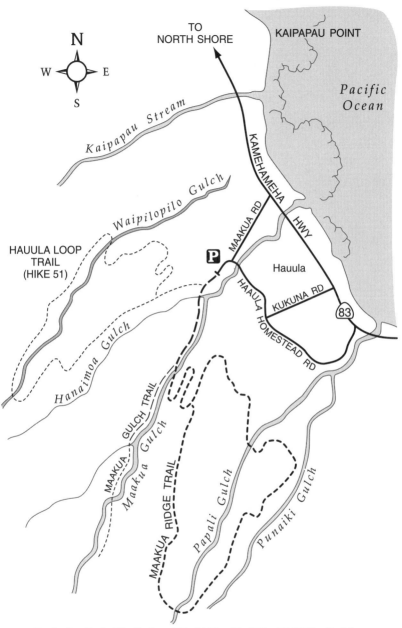

MAAKUA RIDGE TRAIL
PAPALI GULCH

Hike 53
Sacred Falls

(Trail has been indefinitely closed due to
a fatal accident caused by falling rocks. Check with
state park department for current conditions.)

Hiking distance: 4 miles round trip
Hiking time: 2 hours
Elevation gain: 500 feet
Maps: U.S.G.S. Hauula
Oahu Reference Maps: Central Oahu/Windward Coast

Summary of hike: Sacred Falls is an 87-foot cataract that plunges through a rock chute into a pool surrounded by large flat rocks (cover photo). The hike is located in Sacred Falls State Park just south of Hauula. The trail begins at the ocean, crosses a wide valley, then heads up a deep and narrow canyon with towering 1,600-foot walls. There are several stream crossings in the gorge, reaching the trail's end at the base of the pool and falls. Use caution, as the area is prone to flash floods.

Driving directions: From Waikiki, take H-1 west 3.5 miles to Likelike Highway (63), and head northeast to the windward coast. After crossing the mountains, there are two driving options. The shorter, more direct route is the Kahekili Highway (83)—turn left (north) off the Likelike Highway at 7.5 miles. The more scenic but longer route is the Kamehameha Highway (836), a half mile further on the Likelike Highway (63). Both 83 and 836 merge together about 4.5 miles up the coast. From this junction drive 13.7 miles northwest to the Sacred Falls parking lot behind a hedge. The lot is 3.5 miles past Kahana Valley State Park between mile markers 22 and 23.

From the town of Haleiwa on the north shore, the trailhead parking lot is 20.8 miles northeast along Highway 83.

Hiking directions: The trail begins across the lawn near the "Flash Flooding" danger sign. Walk across the large, flat grassy area on the cane road for 1.2 miles, paralleling Kaluanui Stream to the end of the road. Take the footpath through the dense forest canopy, following Kaluanui Stream into the canyon. Pass several large boulders to the first stream crossing. Wade carefully across the stream to the east bank, and continue up the narrowing steep-walled gorge. Follow the cascading watercourse surrounded by lush vegetation. Recross the stream, reaching the base of Sacred Falls and the pool in a mossy, fern-filled grotto. Return along the same route.

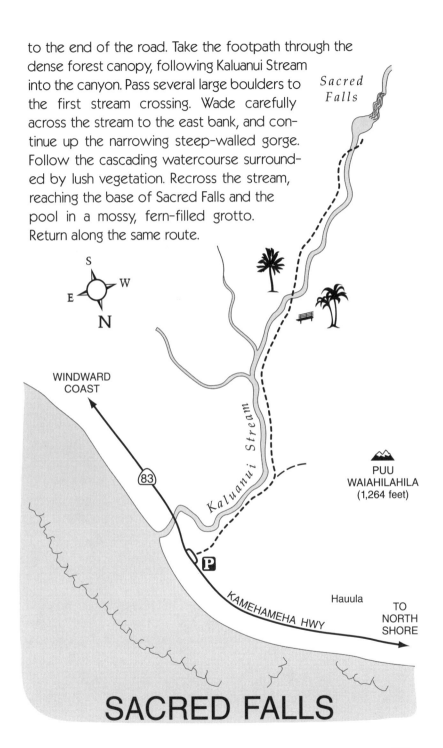

Sacred Falls

S
W
E
N

WINDWARD COAST

83

Kaluanui Stream

PUU WAIAHILAHILA (1,264 feet)

P

KAMEHAMEHA HWY

Hauula

TO NORTH SHORE

SACRED FALLS

Hike 54
Kahana Bay

Hiking distance: 1.4 miles round trip
Hiking time: 45 minutes
Elevation gain: Level
Maps: U.S.G.S. Kahana
         Oahu Reference Maps: Central Oahu/Windward Coast

Summary of hike: Kahana Bay is a scenic tree-lined bay surrounded by steep fluted cliffs of the Koolau Range. The deep bay curves between Mahie Point and Kaluapuleho Point. Kahana Stream flows through the rain-soaked Kahana Valley (Hike 56) into the bay, forming historic Huilua Fishpond, a national landmark and popular swimming hole. This hike follows the bay's sandy shoreline throughout the eight-acre beach park.

Driving directions: From Waikiki, take H-1 west 3.5 miles to Likelike Highway (63), and head northeast to the windward coast. After crossing the mountains, there are two driving options. The shorter, more direct route is the Kahekili Highway (83)—turn left (north) off the Likelike Highway at 7.5 miles. The more scenic but longer route is the Kamehameha Highway (836), a half mile further on the Likelike Highway (63). Both 83 and 836 merge together about 4.5 miles up the coast. From this junction drive 10.2 miles northwest on Highway 83 to Kahana Bay between mile markers 25 and 26. Park in the lot on the right, across from the Kahana Valley State Park entrance.

From the town of Haleiwa on the north shore, Kahana Bay is 24.3 miles northeast along Highway 83.

Hiking directions: Begin the hike at the center of Kahana Bay in a grove of ironwood trees. Bear to the left (northwest) to a lava rock wall and Kapaeleele Boat Ramp at the west end of the bay. Return to the right and walk east through the shady tree grove to a residential home. Follow the hard-packed sand along the curvature of the shoreline to Huilua Fishpond at the mouth of Kahana Stream.

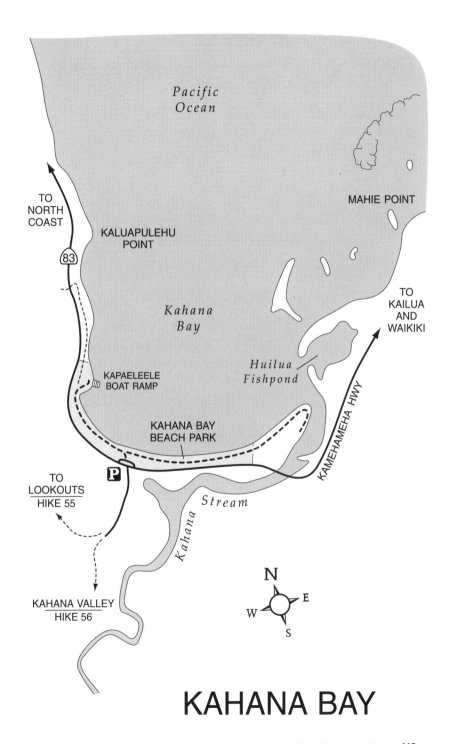

Pacific
Ocean

TO
NORTH
COAST

(83)

KALUAPULEHU
POINT

Kahana
Bay

KAPAELEELE
BOAT RAMP

KAHANA BAY
BEACH PARK

MAHIE POINT

TO
KAILUA
AND
WAIKIKI

Huilua
Fishpond

KAMEHAMEHA HWY

P

TO
LOOKOUTS
HIKE 55

Kahana   Stream

KAHANA VALLEY
HIKE 56

N
W   E
S

KAHANA BAY

Hike 55
Kapaeleele Koa and Keaniani Kilo Lookouts
Kahana Valley State Park

Hiking distance: 1.2 mile loop
Hiking time: 45 minutes
Elevation gain: 150 feet
Maps: U.S.G.S. Kahana
Oahu Reference Maps: Central Oahu/Windward Coast

Summary of hike: This short loop hike leads to Kapaeleele Koa and Keaniani Kilo, two ancient Hawaiian fishing shrines on the oceanfront cliffs high above Kahana Bay. The trail, maintained by the local Boy Scouts, is at the mouth of Kahana Valley and returns along the sandy shoreline in Kahana Bay.

Driving directions: From Waikiki, take H-1 west 3.5 miles to Likelike Highway (63), and head northeast to the windward coast. After crossing the mountains, there are two driving options. The shorter, more direct route is the Kahekili Highway (83)—turn left (north) off the Likelike Highway at 7.5 miles. The more scenic but longer route is the Kamehameha Highway (836), a half mile further on the Likelike Highway (63). Both 83 and 836 merge together about 4.5 miles up the coast. From this junction drive 10.2 miles northwest on Highway 83 to Kahana Bay between mile markers 25 and 26. Turn left at the Kahana Valley State Park sign. Park by the orientation center on the right.

From the town of Haleiwa on the north shore, Kahana Bay is 24.3 miles northeast along Highway 83.

Hiking directions: Walk past the orientation center on the grassy path to the posted Kapaeleele Trailhead. Head into the forest and begin climbing the cliffs along the base of Puu Piei to vistas across Kahana Bay. The path reaches Kapaeleele Koa, a fenced shrine with offerings where fishermen pray for a good catch. Continue traversing the hillside to a posted T-junction. Take the left fork for a short, steep detour to Keaniani Kilo, which means "sparkling lookout." From this fenced shrine are fantastic views of the bay. Return to the main trail, and continue the loop to the left, zigzagging down the steep cliff to a ditch near the highway. Cross the highway and bear right on the sandy beach in Kahana Bay. Recross the highway at the state park entrance, returning to the parking lot.

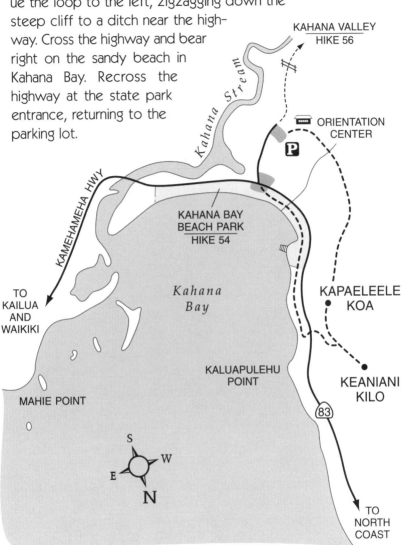

KAPAELEELE KOA and KEANIANI KILO LOOKOUTS
KAHANA VALLEY STATE PARK

Hike 56
Nakoa Trail
Kahana Valley State Park

Hiking distance: 5 mile loop
Hiking time: 3 hours
Elevation gain: 300 feet
Maps: U.S.G.S. Kahana
Oahu Reference Maps: Central Oahu/Windward Coast

Summary of hike: The Nakoa Trail, located in Kahana Valley State Park, leads through a lush vegetated rainforest to a large and deep swimming hole by a dam. The wildland valley is among the wettest valleys on Oahu with as much as 300 inches of rain annually. Kahana Stream flows from the Koolau Mountains through the valley and empties into Kahana Bay.

Driving directions: Follow the driving directions for Hike 55.

Hiking directions: From the Orientation Center, follow the main road up Kahana Valley, passing residential homes and covered shelters. Go around a locked gate that restricts vehicles to a road split. Stay to the right on the main road, reaching another junction by a hunter check-in station at 1.25 miles. The left fork leads directly to the pool. Take the right fork and begin the loop, passing through another locked gate to a water tank. Follow the contours of the hillside with sweeping views of Kahana Valley and the bay. Cross two small tributary streams to a junction just before reaching Kahana Stream. Bear left, then descend and cross Kahana Stream. At the next junction, take a sharp left. Descend from the ridge along the terraced slopes to the pool at Kahana Stream. Cross the small dam to complete the loop. Take the road to the right, back to the parking lot.

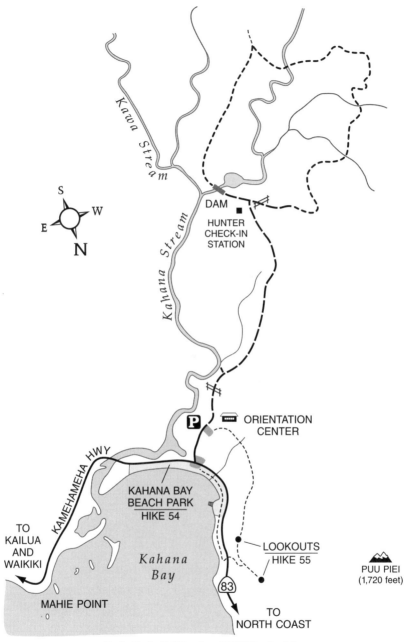

NAKOA TRAIL
KAHANA VALLEY STATE PARK

Hike 57
Kualoa Regional Park

Hiking distance: 2.2 miles round trip
Hiking time: 1 hour
Elevation gain: Level
Maps: U.S.G.S. Kahana
Oahu Reference Maps: Central Oahu/Windward Coast

Summary of hike: Kualoa Regional Park, at the north end of Kaneohe Bay, is surrounded by the spectacular green wall of the Koolau Mountains. The scenic 150-acre park fronts Mokolii "Chinaman's Hat" Island, lying a short 500 yards offshore. The park has a large grassy picnic area with scattered ironwood and wiliwili groves. Paved paths meander through the park to Apua Fishpond and the ancient Molii Pond.

Driving directions: From Waikiki, take H-1 west 3.5 miles to Likelike Highway (63), and head northeast to the windward coast. After crossing the mountains, there are two driving options. The shorter, more direct route is the Kahekili Highway (83)—turn left (north) off the Likelike Highway at 7.5 miles. The more scenic but longer route is the Kamehameha Highway (836), a half mile further on the Likelike Highway (63). Both 83 and 836 merge together about 4.5 miles up the coast. From this junction drive 5.4 miles northwest to the signed Kualoa Regional Park turnoff between mile markers 30 and 31. Turn right and park in the half-mile long lot.

From the town of Haleiwa on the north shore, Kualoa Regional Park is 29 miles northeast along Highway 83.

Hiking directions: Take a paved path or cross the grassy lawn area to the shoreline. Follow the perimeter to Kualoa Point. At low tide, people frequently wade across the submerged reef from Kualoa Point to Chinaman's Hat. Beyond the point, the coastline continues west past the small Apua Fishpond to Molii Pond and a sand spit. The hard-packed sand makes for easy walking. Explore along your own route.

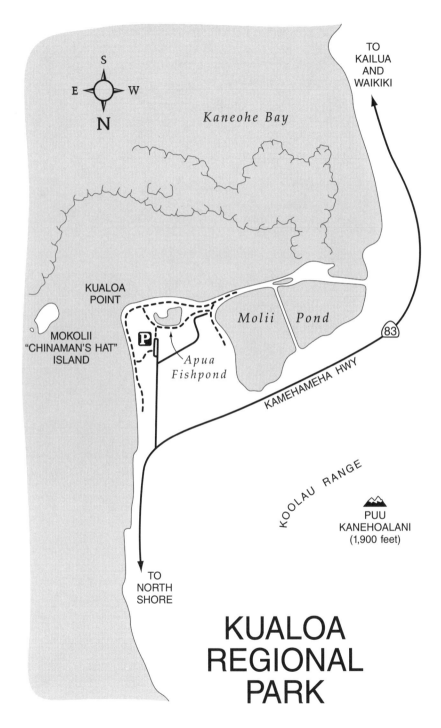

S E · W N (compass)

Kaneohe Bay

TO KAILUA AND WAIKIKI

KUALOA POINT

MOKOLII "CHINAMAN'S HAT" ISLAND

P

Apua Fishpond

Molii Pond

83

KAMEHAMEHA HWY

KOOLAU RANGE

PUU KANEHOALANI (1,900 feet)

TO NORTH SHORE

KUALOA REGIONAL PARK

Other Day Hike Guidebooks

These books may be purchased at your local bookstore or outdoor shop. Or, order them direct from the distributor:

The Globe Pequot Press
246 Goose Lane · P.O. Box 480 · Guilford, CT 06437-0480
www.globe-pequot.com

800-243-0495

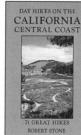

DAY HIKES ON THE
CALIFORNIA
CENTRAL COAST

71 GREAT HIKES
ROBERT STONE

DAY HIKES ON THE
California
Southern
Coast

99 GREAT HIKES
Robert Stone

DAY HIKES AROUND
MONTEREY
& CARMEL

77 GREAT HIKES
ROBERT STONE

DAY HIKES AROUND
BIG SUR

80 GREAT HIKES
ROBERT STONE

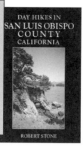

DAY HIKES IN
SAN LUIS OBISPO
COUNTY
CALIFORNIA

ROBERT STONE

DAY HIKES AROUND
SANTA
BARBARA

82 GREAT HIKES
ROBERT STONE

DAY HIKES AROUND
Ventura
County

82 GREAT HIKES
Robert Stone
3rd EDITION

LOS ANGELES TIMES BESTSELLER
DAY HIKES AROUND
Los
Angeles

82 GREAT HIKES
Robert Stone
4th EDITION

DAY HIKES IN
YOSEMITE
NATIONAL PARK

55 GREAT HIKES
ROBERT STONE

DAY HIKES IN
SEQUOIA
AND
KINGS CANYON
NATIONAL PARKS

ROBERT STONE

DAY HIKES IN
YELLOWSTONE
NATIONAL PARK

54 GREAT HIKES
ROBERT STONE

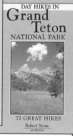

DAY HIKES IN
Grand
Teton
NATIONAL PARK

72 GREAT HIKES
Robert Stone
4th EDITION

DAY HIKES IN THE
BEARTOOTH
MOUNTAINS

RED LODGE, MONTANA TO
YELLOWSTONE NATIONAL PARK
ROBERT STONE

DAY HIKES AROUND
BOZEMAN
MONTANA

INCLUDING THE GALLATIN
CANYON AND PARADISE VALLEY
ROBERT STONE

DAY HIKES AROUND
Missoula
MONTANA

INCLUDING THE BITTERROOTS
AND THE SEELEY-SWAN VALLEY
Robert Stone
3rd EDITION

DAY HIKES ON
Oahu

57 GREAT HIKES
Robert Stone
3rd EDITION

DAY HIKES ON
MAUI

55 GREAT HIKES
ROBERT STONE

DAY HIKES ON
Kauai

55 GREAT HIKES
Robert Stone
2nd EDITION

DAY TRIPS ON
ST. MARTIN

ROBERT STONE

DAY HIKES IN
SEDONA
ARIZONA

25 FAVORITE HIKES
ROBERT STONE

Notes

About the Author

For more than a decade, veteran hiker Robert Stone has been writer, photographer, and publisher of Day Hike Books. Robert resides summers in the Rocky Mountains of Montana and winters on the California Central Coast. This year-round temperate climate enables him to hike throughout the year. When not hiking, Robert is researching, writing, and mapping the hikes before returning to the trails. He is an active member of OWAC (Outdoor Writers Association of California). Robert has hiked every trail in the Day Hike Book series. With over twenty hiking guides in the series, he has hiked over a thousand trails throughout the western United States and Hawaii.